CW00642917

# THE SUFFOLK COAST

## RUSSELL EDWARDS

TERENCE DALTON LIMITED
LAVENHAM    .    SUFFOLK
1991

# THE SUFFOLK COAST

Published by
TERENCE DALTON LIMITED

ISBN 0 86138 054 1

*Text photoset in 10/12pt Baskerville*

*Printed in Great Britain at*
*The Lavenham Press Limited, Lavenham, Suffolk*

# Contents

## DEDICATION

To
Daniel and Kate
our grandchildren
May they long continue to appreciate the joys of their
Suffolk countryside

# Acknowledgements

I AM most grateful to the Oxford University Press for permission to publish an extract from Thomas Tusser's *Five Hundred Points of Good Husbandry*, and to Ruth Fuller, Warrenton Page's daughter, for permission to quote an extract from her father's book *Holbrook*. I acknowledge with pleasure and thanks the assistance given me by Philip Willis, Stutton's local historian, Mrs Bence-Jones for her help in writing about Colonel Tomline, Doreen Rayner for her knowledge of Felixstowe, and Frank Hussey, who unstintingly made his research on Landguard Fort available to me.

Major Eustace Miller gave me much information about life at Bawdsey Manor and I am grateful to the Commander of the RAF station at Bawdsey for laying on a conducted tour and allowing me to take photographs.

Michael Weaver, local historian, advised me on Woodbridge and special thanks go to Valerie Fenwick, who told me of the excavations she was undertaking on Burrow Hill, Butley, and checked the relevant part of the manuscript. My thanks to the late Richard Pinney and William Pinney for their advice on oyster, salmon and all other fish, John Partridge for introducing me to Havergate Island and to Bob and Dot Ling for relating to me their work at Snape Maltings.

Dr Pickard, curator of the Dunwich Museum, was kind enough to check my manuscript on Dunwich and to give permission for quoting James Bird's poem "The Dunwich Rose". My thanks to Monica Phillips for teaching me about amber and also to Rachel Massey and Glyn Evans of the Chillesford Local History Museum. I am also grateful to the numerous people who kindly gave permission to take photographs.

I would like to pay tribute to my wife, Gee, for her infinite patience and for accompanying me on many jaunts and for doing lots of different tasks associated with getting out a book. Finally my very grateful thanks to Natalie Wheatley for editing the manuscript.

Without the help of so many people the writing of such a book would be difficult, and if there are any mistakes, which I hope there are not, they will be mine, and mine alone.

# Introduction

THE SUFFOLK coast is an area of outstanding natural beauty, a blend of beaches—shingle and sand—edged by a mixture of marsh and heathland, behind which spreads a patchwork of forests and farms dotted with picturesque villages, their origins deep in history.

In 1974 the Countryside Commission designated thirty-four miles of this coastline as a Heritage Coast, from Kessingland in the north to Bawdsey ferry in the south. There are forty such areas of coastline around England and Wales, nominated to protect the wildlife and its environment, whilst improving recreational amenities and public access without, one hopes, destroying the beauty and tranquillity.

Extending the whole length of the Suffolk Heritage Coast Way is a continuous system of public footpaths marked by yellow arrows or bands on wayside signs, which make it possible to explore even the remotest parts of this area without making recourse to roads.

I first became aware of the coastal path when my daughter, then sixteen, joined the Suffolk Constabulary and was required, along with her colleagues, to complete the coastal walk in three days, carrying tents and equipment with them as part of an adventure training programme. The cadets, along with other youth organizations, volunteers and young persons from the job creation schemes, did maintenance work along the coast under the direction of the Heritage Coast warden. The work included clearing litter, most of which comes from ships dumping it at sea, restoring paths, making stiles, erecting fences, building steps down sandy cliffs, renovating cliff falls, creating car parks and manning information centres. I am not sure exactly how much work my daughter actually achieved, as she fell in love with the Heritage Coast warden's son, Mark. They eventually married and now they, with our two grandchildren Daniel and Kate, relish the amenities their paternal grandfather had so carefully nurtured for us all.

In December, 1984, Babergh District Council announced their Shotley Peninsula Countryside Plan, whose objectives are similar to those of a Heritage Coast. There is a public right of way which, except for one short break at Stutton on the Stour, extends right around the peninsula from the Essex boundary at Cattawade on the River Stour to the Strand along the River Orwell, passing in front of my home at Holbrook where I have lived for over thirty years. The Suffolk coast suddenly became a family affair and it became a challenge to try to walk its seventy-mile length using the public rights of way. Only in three short distances did my wife and I have to resort to roads; at Felixstowe Dock, where the public footpath has been enveloped by the container port, between Hemley and Martlesham Creek, where the sea wall has been breached by the floods of 1953, and from the Orwell Bridge to the Nacton shore, where there is access but no public right of way.

Advancing years inhibited us from emulating our daughter and her friends from walking the distance in a few days, although we envied them. Our strategy was more leisurely. We would drive to a location near to a footpath we were exploring, walk until we reached a charming and convenient hostelry, where we would enjoy lunch accompanied by some energy restoring beverage (beer), and then return by the same or a circular route, marking off the distances covered on our Ordnance Survey map. This book has evolved from those coastal walks. It is not a collection of routes (these are clearly marked as red dots on the OS maps) but a miscellany of stories and events we have gathered during our exploration of Suffolk's Heritage Coast.

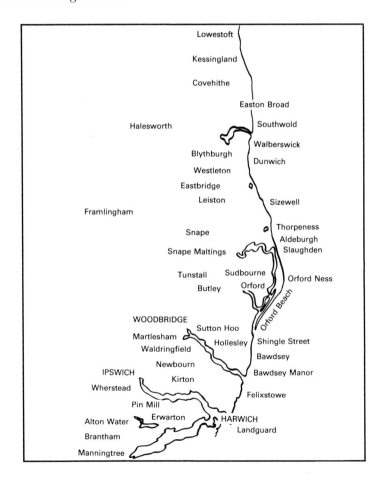

CHAPTER ONE

# From Cattawade to the Orwell Bridge

W E BEGAN our perambulations around the south Suffolk coast at Cattawade, where a quaint eighteenth-century hump-backed, brick bridge with three arches spans the River Stour. This, and the railway bridge, joins Suffolk with Essex. A previous bridge dates back to the middle of the thirteenth century when the Bishop of Norwich, Walter de Suffield, gave two marks towards its upkeep. A hundred years later its warden applied for and was granted a plot of land forty-eight feet by a hundred feet (worth a ha'penny a year) near to the causeway, on which to build a chapel dedicated to the Virgin Mary:

> In which to celebrate the divine offices everyday for ever, for the King and all the benefactors of the bridge and causy.

At about the same time a hermit living in Cattawade was given permission to beg for alms to pay for bridge repairs. The church was still there in the sixteenth century when Robert Debnam was hanged on Cattaway Causeway:

> Within the sight of the old chapel of St Mary *ad pontem* erected by the Rector of East Bergholt in 1291.

He, along with three others, had broken into the church at Dovercourt and had stolen the crucifix from above the rood screen and burnt it on Dovercourt Green. The crucifix was alleged to have miraculous powers and brought a steady income from pilgrims for the church.

Daniel Defoe records sending his horses by way of a wooden bridge at Cattawade in 1724 during his tour of the eastern counties, while he sensibly took a boat up the River Orwell to reach Ipswich. It seems that the wooden structure was in need of constant repair and positively dangerous to cross on foot or horseback, particularly if a coach was coming the other way, as the carriageway was less than eight feet across. It was rebuilt in 1791 at a cost of £500 by a carpenter, William Jeffrey, who made such a good job of it that he was given a £21 bonus, but by 1858 it had again become derelict and dangerous.

It was about this time that the Stour traffic was at its busiest, the river having been made navigable as far as Sudbury, from where the horsedrawn barges,

**Opposite:** The yellow arrow points the way to the Heritage coast.

which feature so prominently in Constable's paintings, brought bricks and grain down river to be shipped to London in Thames sailing barges. The horses were unharnessed at Brantham Lock, just above the bridge, while the barges were punted under the bridge and made their way , with help from a makeshift sail, across the estuary to Mistley. As late as 1931 Len Pattle, who lived opposite the bridge at Braham Hall, remembers watching the horses leaping off the barges from one towpath to the other and galloping down the road for their fodder, which had been placed in their stables to encourage them home.

Four hundred years ago Thomas Tusser occupied Braham Hall and farmed the land beside the Stour, where he is reputed to have grown the first barley in this district. However it does seem likely that barley was grown here before his time. Perhaps he grew better crops by adding manure to this sandy soil. He wrote in his book *Five Hundred Points of Good Husbandry*:

> In Brantham, where rie but no barlie did growe,
> good barlie I had, as a meany did knowe.
> Five seame of an aker I truely was paid,
> for thirty loade muck of each aker so laid.

Tusser was only the second person by 1557 to have written a book on farming (the first edition was *A Hundred Points of Good Husbandry*, which he later extended to "Five Hundred" adding advice on keeping a wife). From his works come quotations in common use today such as:

> Don't buy a pig in poke.
> Fools and their money are soon parted.
> It's an ill wind that blows nobody any good.
> A rolling stone gathers no moss.

Tusser was born at Rivenhall in Essex, the youngest of five children. His fine singing voice was his passport for an education at St Paul's, where he was a chorister. Later, at Eton, he suffered a severe beating of fifty-three strokes:

> For fault but small, or none at all.

He then went to Trinity College, Cambridge, from where he became Lord Paget's musician for ten years. He married, took up farming and brought his bride to Cattawade, where he wrote his first book. The damp from the river made his wife ill, so they moved to Ipswich:

> A towne of price, like paradise.

His wife died and he remarried, continuing to farm in Norfolk before taking up music again in Norwich Cathedral. His Essex farming was unsuccessful; he was mostly in London, then in Cambridge to avoid the London Plague, and finally returned to London to die in a debtor's prison in May 1580. There is a memorial plaque in Manningtree Church, to which Tusser brought his wife by boat, as she was too ill to walk up the hill to their church at Brantham.

A later nineteenth-century occupant of Braham Hall was Henry Page, whose son Frederick was alleged to have murdered Fanny Clarke, a young girl of twenty-four who was a domestic servant at Church House Farm in Brantham (now Brantham Place), where she was found dying of gunshot wounds. The inquest was held at the Bull Inn; a love triangle between the girl, Frederick and his brother Robert was a possible cause of the incident. Frederick was sent to Broadmoor, where he was diagnosed as a schizophrenic; he died there on 28th August, 1886. He was thirty. The incident still provides a melodrama for local theatricals and has recently provided the story for a film.

There is no direct access from Cattawade Bridge onto the coastal path, which is reached by taking the narrow road past the main factory entrances and following the path from the car park to Decoy Pond, a popular fishing spot. The British Xylonite factory (now Wardle-Storey) moved to its present site beside the Stour in 1887 from its factory in Hackney, London, where it had manufactured plastic shirt fronts, collars and cuffs, popular in Victorian times as they did not require laundering. They also made combs and keyboards from the same material—celluloid (a mixture of nitro-cellulose and camphor)—which could, happily, be made to look like ivory or tortoiseshell. The main factory gates has an emblem which depicts the tortoise and the elephant saved from wholesale slaughter and possible extinction by the advent of plastic materials. (Plastic spectacle frames are still made with a tortoiseshell design.)

Braham Hall at Cattawade. The relatively modern exterior conceals an earlier timber-framed building. Thomas Tusser lived and farmed here in the sixteenth century.

The neat, square tower of Brantham Church with its ornate weather vane came into view on my left as I walked up the hill beside the railway embankment away from the dark and dismal Decoy Pond. The Reverend Durande Rhudde was appointed to the Living at Brantham along with those of Great Wenham and East Bergholt in 1782. It was his granddaughter Elizabeth Maria Bicknell who, after considerable opposition from her grandfather who disowned her and removed her name from his Will, married John Constable, a local artist and the most revered of our English landscape painters. Their difficult and prolonged courtship lasted over seven years before they were married in St Martin-in-the-Fields in 1816 without members of either family being present.

Prior to his courtship with Maria, his relationship with the domineering Dr Rhudde must have been cordial, as he painted a picture of "Christ Blessing Little Children" in 1805 for the reredos of Brantham church. It is now in Christchurch Mansion. According to local tradition the faces of the people in this picture are those of some of Constable's family. When I asked John Constable (the great-great-grandson of the painter) about this, he suggested that the lady on the extreme right could be that of the artist's sister Mary, and having seen a picture of Constable's two sisters, Anne and Mary, painted in 1814, I wondered if the

Brantham church. This church once contained a painting by John Constable entitled "Christ Blessing the Little Children". It can now be seen in the Ipswich Museum.

girl next to Mary with the veil over her head in the Brantham picture was Constable's sister Anne. D. S. MacColl, writing in the *Burlington Magazine* of 1923, stated, without evidence, that John Lewis, a child from Dedham, was the model for the infant held by Christ. It is known that Constable had painted portraits of the Lewis sisters.

I did not follow the official footpath, as it does not go all the way down the hill but bears left past a demolished barn, over the stile, and follows the marsh hedge to join the sea wall at the bottom of Brantham Hall Lane. The farmer prefers people to use the path which joins the lane from Brantham Church and follows it over the railway bridge and down the hill, close to the barbed wire fence which leads to the sea wall. A precariously placed plank in the reeds affords a safe, dry, summer crossing over the ditch and up on to the coastal path, which runs eastwards along the sea wall past a pretty pink-painted house. Part of this private residence was once the miller's house belonging to a tidal mill, known as Stutton New Mills (plural presumably because throughout the ages there had been several mills on this site), demolished in 1908. In that year Vincent Redstone wrote in his *Memorials of Old Suffolk*:

> It is a lonely and desolate spot, the only tidal mill on the river, "God-forsaken and man-forsaken"; the curlew whistles overhead; the cry of the peewit is always there.

A flock of curlew flew along the river's edge and peewits did fly up from the adjoining fields as I walked by, but God-forsaken—never, if He is anywhere it is here in this isolated peaceful paradise.

Beyond the pink house a short length of the path was overgrown with tall slippery grasses and I made recourse to the shore before walking through a plantation of trees on the edge of the Stutton Hall Estate (an Elizabethan timber framed Hall built in 1553) and along the sandy cliff top to Stutton Ness. There is no public access along the shore beyond this point, so I turned inland to take the path past Crepping Hall to Stutton village. Crepping Hall has a history going back to the thirteenth century, when it was the property of William de Creppinge. During the reign of Henry VIII it was granted to Humphrey Wingfield, a member of the famous Suffolk family. In 1890 they sank a fifteen-hundred-foot shaft to find a coal seam which, it was believed, went under the Stour to Harwich. Thank goodness the project was abandoned and the village left to its quiet agrarian ways. The King's Head, an old coaching inn, reputed to be the haunt of poachers and smugglers, its historic ambience unmarred by modern plastic adornment, is as cosy and hospitable today as it was when old Nat Dale served purl (spiced ale) back in 1851:

> Good people stop and pray walk in,
> Here's foreign brandy, rum and gin;
> And what is more, good purl and ale
> Are both sold here by old Nat Dale.

The King's Head at Stutton.

At the turn of the century Mr Gladwell was the landlord and also the local coalman. Beer was then one penny a pint and coal eighteen pence a hundredweight. Families were large in those days: he had eight children, who had to go to bed at five o'clock before the pub opened for the evening. But for a treat, on Saturday evenings, they were allowed to sing to the customers in the "big room".

In 1978 the Tattingstone valley, which lies immediately behind Stutton village, was flooded to make the Alton Water reservoir to provide an additional supply for Ipswich. A dam was constructed of London clay, sand and gravel dug out from the valley bottom, and the reservoir was filled with water pumped four miles through pipes from the River Gipping at Sproughton. Alton Water covers 399 acres, has a maximum depth of fifty-nine feet and holds two thousand million gallons of water, from which Ipswich draws fifteen hundred million gallons a day to add to the thirteen million it pumps from its bore holes. It has been developed into an attractive amenity area and is the first reservoir in Britain to be stocked for coarse fishing, containing tench, roach, bream, rudd, perch, pike, carp and eel. Other activities include sailing, rowing and sub-aqua diving, and there is a pleasant eight-mile country walk around the reservoir with attractive picnic places.

Alton Hall was demolished to make way for the reservoir but Alton Mill, together with the mill house, was removed from the valley and reassembled at the rural life museum in Stowmarket. The mill is an attractive, three-storeyed weatherboarded structure. It has an internal overshoot waterwheel that drives three millstones. Mr Blackmore was the miller at the turn of the century and his daughter Agnes and five other children were born in the adjoining mill house. She told me about her childhood at the mill and in the valley.

She said that the farmers would arrive with their carts of grain early in the morning. Once they had attached a noose to their two-hundredweight sacks she would use the rope and pulley to hoist them up to the top floor. Here along with the other children she would stand in the storage bins (dark, dusty, dangerous places where the risk of suffocation from falling grain was always present), and feed the grain through a hole in the floor to the millstones below. As a miller her father earned about a pound a week but he was also one of the best stone dressers in the county. (Dressing the millstones involved cutting fine radial grooves in the stones along which the flour travelled to the periphery, where it was collected and bagged.) There were no fixed working hours for a miller, as they worked "to the tune of the water". That is they worked the mill continuously while there was sufficient water in the pond to drive the machinery. Sometimes a neighbour upstream would divert the water for his own purpose and Agnes was then despatched to negotiate the resumption of the water supply from the lake in Tattingstone park. The mill was working until 1947 and helped to feed the people through two world wars. Agnes married the village postman, Fred Rogers, who walked from Holbrook to deliver mail to the mill and then continued on foot through the valley to Bentley station to meet the mail train from London. Appropriately Agnes became the village postmistress at Holbrook for many years. She always maintained that Alton Mill was haunted by the ghost of a man who got trapped under the mill wheel, and I heard another story that unwanted babies were disposed of beneath the wheel. Whether the ghost of Alton Mill is now in residence at Stowmarket is not known.

I wonder what Squire Edward White would think of the view from his former bedroom window at Tattingstone Place, his eighteenth-century mansion which now stands almost on the water's edge. It was he who built the Tattingstone Wonder—three terraced cottages disguised as a church, built about 1750 or possibly 1790. The squire required cottages for his estate workers but he also wanted to see a church from his bedroom window and solved the problem by building the Wonder. Arthur Mee has the story that the squire said people wondered about nothing so he would give them something to wonder about!

I returned to the coastal footpath at Holbrook Creek by walking the back road (Lower Street) to Stutton church, passing on the way a quaint country cottage, its walls elaborately pargeted with a design of vines and the words Ancient House over the door. According to local historian Philip Willis, the

7

cottage, also used as a maltings, was restored in the early seventeenth century at the same time as the much pargeted Ancient House in Ipswich.

Stutton church stands a mile or so from its village, where Stutton once stood before it was burnt down to halt the spread of the Plague. Ken Seacome, historian and late colleague, was unable to find any direct evidence for this locally held view. An entry in the church records reveals:

> Thomas, first son of William Lord Fairfax and Viscount Emeley Dame Elizabeth, wife, baptised July 23 1646.

A small Norman window reset in the east wall of the vestry dates the earliest part of the church and overlooks the last resting place of my parents. From here I went round the church and through a copse and onto the drift, a gently sloping hill, whose soil contains the phosphate remains of those who died from the Plague. Here is the best view of the Stour estuary, the path leading down to Markwell's Farm in the foreground, the eye seeking out the passenger ships at Parkeston and Harwich beyond the river.

Markwell's Farm stands across the old parish boundary between Stutton and Holbrook. A mark on an old beam denotes the boundary within the farmhouse. It was adjudged that a person who slept with his head in Stutton and his feet in Holbrook was a resident of Stutton.

Between the farm and Holbrook Creek the fields of the Royal Hospital School slope gently down to the river. It is over thirty years now since I took the bus out of Ipswich to attend an interview for the post of science master at the school. I wondered then if I would be taking a single journey back to the station or whether the passing Suffolk scene would become a familiarity. Sometimes I have been tempted to seek new pastures but could find nowhere with this scenic beauty, with the excellent facilities of the school but most of all with boys who on the whole are friendly, courteous and willing to learn. It was a tonic to come here after two years' teaching on Merseyside.

The Royal Hospital School is a comprehensive boarding school, originally for the sons of seafarers but now open to all children, boys and girls, between eleven and eighteen years. It is part of Greenwich Hospital, which was established by Queen Mary and King William in 1694 for the relief and support of seamen who, by reason of age, wounds or other disabilities were incapable of further service at sea, and also for the maintenance and education of their children. The school was established in 1712 to fulfil the latter need and was housed in the Queen's House at Greenwich where it became famous for its teaching of navigation. In 1933 the school was transferred from Greenwich to its present site overlooking the Stour at Holbrook. It was built on the 850-acre estate of Gifford Sherman Reade, a tea merchant, who gave it to the Admiralty with a considerable amount of his fortune in gratitude for not losing any of his tea ships during the First World War. The mosaic in the lady chapel of the school chapel was built in his memory.

Over the main west door of the chapel presides the statue of St Nicholas, the patron saint of the Navy and of children, but its features are those of Arthur Smallwood, the Director of the Greenwich Hospital, whose idea it was to move the school to the Holbrook estate. Construction of the impressive Neo-Georgian school building commenced in 1928 during the unhappy period of the great Depression. Warrenton Page, a native of Holbrook, recalls the scene:

> Most of the work was hard manual labour, and for those who had been unemployed for a long period it was impossible to keep up with the pace that the gangers set. In spite of working very hard for two hours or more, a two minute rest could be the cause of instant dismissal. The brick rubble that was used for road making was brought into Holbrook creek by sailing barges. The rubble was then transferred to lorries, and this was particularly hard work, done with bare hands and shovels, and several men collapsed and had to leave the job.

The foundation stone was laid by the Duke of York (later to become King George VI) on 26th October, 1928, and under it was placed a copy of that day's *East Anglian Daily Times* together with a set of newly minted coins. The boys occupied the completed buildings in the autumn of 1933. Queen Mary visited the school in 1938 and gave two trees (turkey oaks costing 7/6d each) and these, with twenty-two donated by members of the Royal Family and other dignitaries, lined the front of the school, which became Queen Mary's Drive. The conifers, through which the path to the creek goes, were planted while James Callaghan (former Prime Minister) was chairman of the school management committee and is affectionately known as Callaghan's copse. It was mostly destroyed in the gales of 1984. In 1968 the Queen Mother was the principal guest at Speech Day when she opened and gave her name to a new school building, which now accommodates science laboratories.

It is a picturesque walk to follow the stream from Holbrook Creek to the mill and then up the hill to the village, where good beer and refreshment can be taken at the Compasses. The construction of Holbrook Church started at the beginning of the fourteenth century either by Richard Holbrook or his son John, who is credited with giving the Living to its first rector, Radulfus de Cretygne. They built an altar tomb to the founder's memory, replaced in 1824 with a fireplace and then by a vestry door over which a trefoil arch, once part of the tomb's canopy, now remains. In the wall is a niche, carved with an effigy, covering a hole in which Mr Phipson, FSA, discovered a small corroded metal vase three parts full of chalk lime and a loamy substance containing small pieces of charcoal. He deduced that the vase contained the remains of a defectively embalmed or cremated heart. (It is known that hearts and sometimes bowels were separately buried from the rest of the body.) He further surmised that if the adjacent tomb was that of the founder of the church, John Holbrook, then the heart was that of his wife or their son, also John, who died in 1317. In 1376 Margery Holbrook married Sir John Fastolf and the Holbrook estates passed to her husband, whose descendant became immortalized as Shakespeare's Falstaff.

The Lady Chapel of the Royal Hospital School at Holbrook.

Holbrook Mill, which ceased grinding corn in 1926. The mill is now a restaurant.

In a corner of the church is the tomb of Judge John Clench. On it reclines his effigy, with that of his daughter-in-law, Margerie, reclining at a more appropriate lower level. John Clench had one of his three residences at Holbrook, now known as Holbrook Gardens. He was the first Recorder of Ipswich and became a judge of the Queen's Bench in the time of Elizabeth I, working the Northern circuit, where, along with Judge Rhodes, he heard the case against Margaret Clitherow and sentenced her to death. She was canonized on 25th October, 1970.

Margaret was a Yorkshire girl, the daughter of Thomas Middleton, a candle-maker. She married John Clitherow, Protestant and rich butcher. They lived together in the Shambles at York. Although brought up a Protestant she converted to the Catholic faith in 1574, four years after Queen Elizabeth was excommunicated. Catholics were then no longer obliged to owe allegiance to the Queen and became traitors against the state and could be charged with treason. At this time Jesuit priests from abroad travelled through England, hiding in priest-holes disguised behind oak panelling in people's homes, and preached spiritual allegiance to the Pope and not Elizabeth. Margaret Clitherow kept two hiding places in York. Some of the priests she hid were martyred; she wished for the same fate and prayed for it to happen under the gibbet at York Tyburn. Her prayers were answered. After a period of imprisonment her house was raided in 1586 by the priest hunters. A Flemish servant boy, threatened with violence, showed them the hiding place, which contained a chalice and vestments for communion. Margaret stood trial before Judge Clench and Judge Rhodes on a charge that she:

Housed priests which was a felony without benefit of clergy.

She refused to plead to the charge so that she would not implicate her children or servants. The severe punishment, a kind of judicial torture, for refusing to plead to a charge was: "Peine forte et dure." She was pressed to death.

Margaret walked barefooted to the tolbooth at Ousebridge, and sent her hose and shoes to her daughter Anne that she might follow in her footsteps. She was laid on the ground with a sharp stone in her back, a door was placed on top of her weighted with stones until she died. It took fifteen minutes. She is deemed to have said:

God be thanked I am not worthy of so good a death as this.

Her body was thrown away but recovered and buried by her friends. Her shrivelled hand is preserved at the Bar Convent, York, and her hair is at the Archbishop's House, Westminster.

A dozen plain and unattractive stones, about twelve inches in diameter with a small hole at each of the their centres, set into the church walls, six on the inside and the others divided equally between the east and west walls outside, remain as Holbrook's mystery consecration stones. Perhaps a cross or a statue was attached to the centre of each stone, over which the Bishop would have poured oil when new parts of the church were blessed and consecrated.

The coastal path continues from Holbrook Creek along the side of the fields edging the river to the Harkstead shore, where sun worshippers make good use of a thin stretch of sand wedged between the fields and the mud. It was hereabouts that the skeletal remains of a giant mammoth were found in the Harkstead brick earth. This extinct elephant was estimated to be between fifteen and twenty years old when it died a hundred thousand years ago, at a time when the country was basking in the sun between two interglacial periods. Its remains now rest in the Ipswich Museum alongside another, which was found at Stutton.

Having descended from the Harkstead sandy cliffs, where an excellent view of the sweeping curve of the Holbrook bay is obtained, I kept close to the edge of the field to avoid crossing the salt marsh criss-crossed with small streams. It was here that I stumbled across a clump of marsh mallow plants resembling an odd looking bunch of nettles, but their pale pink flowers and down covered leaves identified this rare plant. It gave its name to those sticky sweets now made from a mixture of gelatin, sugar and starch but originally made from water and mucilage (a gluey mixture of carbohydrates) extracted from the marsh mallow roots. The plant was much used in early medicine. According to the nineteenth century herbalist Culpeper (who cured his son of the bloody flux, a plague of the guts, by giving him marsh mallows boiled in milk), root of marsh mallow boiled in wine cures coughs, hoarseness, shortage of breath and swellings in women's breasts and was used extensively in poultices to reduce inflammation and hard swellings and to ease pain in any part of the body. Hippocrates is said to have given it to those injured in battle and applied it to their wounds while in France, where the plant is common. The dried roots were chewed by teething babies so that the mucilage would soothe their gums and stomachs.

Beyond Harkstead the way was blocked by what at first seemed to be an impenetrable high hedge but, by going to the left, I found a way through it to the remains of Palace Quay on the shore. Erwarton Quay is next along from the Palace with Johnny-All-Alone between them: a pool of water surrounded by reeds defended from the sea by a concrete dam. No-one seems to know who Johnny was and why he was all alone, but Edward Wrinch suggested he may have been Johnny Shilling from Harkstead, who lived in a boat off shore. At the pool I watched two stoats approach through the long grass, popping up occasionally to peer over it, their heads rotating like periscopes. They crept through the reeds to the water's edge, where, with a darting action, they thrust a forepaw into the water in an attempt to catch moorhen chicks, which teased the stoats by swimming just out of reach and then returned to the bank when they thought it was safe, only to be attacked again. The stoats were persistent but unsuccessful and eventually skulked away.

Erwarton Ness has been associated for generations with the Wrinch family. Late last century local farmers owned seven spritsail barges: *Victoria, Farmer's Boy, Snowdrop, Butterfly, Primrose, Bluebell* and *Prince Donna*—all stackies, having broad decks on which to stack the hay. They sailed to all the hards (roadways built into the river along which the farm carts or tumbrils could go at low tide, day or night, to load and unload), the farm quays and jetties along the Stour estuary, Stutton Mill, Stutton Point, New Found Out at Markwell's Farm, Holbrook Creek, Palace Quay and Erwarton to collect farm produce, hay, straw, mangolds and grain and take it to London to feed the population, the cab horses and the dairy herds. Hay bales were built into stacks on the broad decks of the barges, overlapping the sides and extending ten feet or more up the mast so that the steersman could not see the way ahead, necessitating the services of the rick skipper on top of the stack to call directions to the mate at the tiller. The mast was lowered into a gap left in the middle of the stack when the barges went under the Thames bridges. Wrinch's also owned the *Cygnet*, which was a much smaller barge having only a twenty-five ton capacity. It was used solely for carrying grain from the local farms to the mills and maltings at Ipswich, Felixstowe and Mistley and has now retired to Pin Mill.

From 1894–1914 grandfather Wrinch leased the Providence Wharf on the Thames, from where he conducted his forage business, obtaining farm produce not only from the farms along the Stour, but also from those along the Orwell, Deben, Alde and the Walton backwaters. This was delivered to London in his barges, which returned to Suffolk with manure and street sweepings to be spread on the land. Unloading the steaming, stenching muck was an arduous day and night business, as laden barges resting on a hard could only be unloaded at low tide. After a couple of hours' toil, the men would relax in the muck in the warm, unpleasant hold to take refreshment, often a substantial meal. The muck was blamed for what was believed to be the last outbreak of the Plague in England, which started at Latimer's Cottages just outside Holbrook in 1910. A Mr Chapman, his wife and daughter all died from this mysterious disease, as also did their home help Mrs Parker. The following year a sailor at HMS Ganges at Shotley contracted the disease, possibly from a rabbit he had killed near Latimer Cottages. He recovered and, although subsequently blinded, he lived to seventy-six. Not so lucky were Mrs Bugg and her next door neighbour, who lived at Warren Lane Cottages, Erwarton. They were the last people to die of the Plague in Suffolk in June 1918.

The barges, not all of them belonging to the Wrinch family, carried other cargoes such as chemicals for the plastics factory at Cattawade, imported corn for the mills, coal for unloading at the coal house wharf at Holbrook, stones for road building and even materials for building the Royal Hospital School.

The sea wall resumes again after Erwarton Ness but the path is overgrown with long grasses and I made my way between the pools and streams in the salt-

The *Cygnet* barge at Pin Mill. It was once used to collect produce from the local farms.

marsh. In the summer months this is covered with sea lavender, which is used in winter floral decorations as the dried flowers retain their colour. Marsh samphire is also abundant. These succulent, many branched, spiky plants were once collected into heaps, rather like hay, and burnt over a large hole into which the soda ash fell. This was used for soap and glass making, which gave rise to its alternative name of glasswort. Cooked samphire looks like soggy spinach and is still considered a local delicacy.

The tower of Erwarton Church stood out framed by the deep gold of the cornfields, and I retraced my steps along a path back from the sea wall to the church . There I watched stone masons repairing the clerestory wall with septaria (stone nodules) which had been collected by local people and brought up from the river mud, as was done when the church was first built. In 1836 stone masons came across a lead box containing black dust. It was immediately linked with the popular local legend that when Anne Boleyn was beheaded at the Tower of London in 1536, her heart was removed and brought to Erwarton, where it was buried in the church wall. It is known that before her marriage to Henry VIII she often visited her aunt, Jane Boleyn, at Erwarton Hall where she lived with her husband Sir Philip Calthorpe. It is said that Henry came to court her there.

The Hall, with its spectacular gateway, is but a few yards along the road towards Shotley, but, more important to the thirsty walker, the appropriately named Queen's Head, an attractive inn, is a few yards away in the opposite direction. Here good sustaining nourishment is very welcome before returning to the river and the remainder of the walk along the fields and through the woods to Shotley.

The Bristol Arms at Shotley, which takes its name from the Marquis of Bristol, the local Lord of the Manor, has splendid views across the river to the passenger ships at Parkeston Quay and Harwich, and is an idyllic spot from which to watch the world go past. The pub was originally called the Ferry Inn and its tenants operated the ferry service to Harwich. Shotley started life as an Anglo-Saxon settlement and saw its first naval engagement in AD 885. An Anglo-Saxon chronicle states:

> The same year King Alfred sent a force from Kent to East Anglia. As soon as they came to the mouth of the Stour they met sixteen Viking ships and fought with them. They seized all the ships and killed all the men.

The battle was fought at Bloody Point, at the tip of the Shotley Peninsula.

King Edward III and his ten-year-old son the Duke of Cornwall (later to be known as the Black Prince) were guests of the Lord of the Manor, Sir Thomas Visdelou, at Old Hall, Shotley, whilst waiting for his fleet to assemble at Harwich harbour, from where he sailed to defeat the French in the English Channel. In 1899 HMS *Ganges*, a three-decker sailing ship, dropped anchor in the Stour off Harwich to be used as a naval training ship. Later a shore establishment was built at Shotley to begin the long association with the Royal Navy, which lasted until 1976. The establishment is now used as a police training centre. The mast manning ceremony was the most spectacular event in the Shotley calendar, when young sailors from *Ganges* climbed the 143-foot mast and one of them stood on top of it on a button measuring just eleven inches across and saluted.

I walked round the tip of Shotley peninsula along King Edward VII Drive (Queen Victoria Drive goes in the opposite direction) and entered the Orwell estuary—the river from which George Orwell took his name—along the sea wall until I came to Crane's Creek, from where an inland path took me to Shotley Church and the naval cemetery overlooking the Orwell estuary.

During the First World War the casualties from ships returning to Harwich after battles in the North Sea were landed at Shotley. The dead were brought to the naval cemetery on gun carriages pulled by boys of HMS *Ganges*. Here are buried the dead from HMS *Amphion*, which was struck by mines while returning from a North Sea patrol in which she had sunk a German minelayer disguised as a hospital ship. There is a memorial to the crews of the submarines *E4* and *E41*, which collided in Harwich harbour, and there are many graves belonging to boys of HMS *Ganges* struck down by the great influenza epidemic of 1918.

The naval cemetery at Shotley.

Major Buckley, a former friend and colleague, is interred in this military cemetery. As aide-de-camp to Winston Churchill he was introduced to Stalin by Churchill as, "My Marine officer, a member of the finest Corps in the world". He was a true representative of the Royal Marine Corps.

Cemeteries have a philosophic effect on me, and it was with a heavy heart that I returned to the river and walked along the sea wall to the small dock at Hare's Creek. I wended my way through the edge of the marshes to Clamp House by Butterman's Bay which took its name from the small, fast, sailing schooners carrying dairy produce from the Channel Isles.

A hundred years ago Butterman's Bay would have made a majestic sight, with triple-masted sailing ships, square riggers and steamers riding at anchor to await the arrival of spritsail barges to relieve them of their cargoes—grain, timber and fertilizers brought from places as far away as South America and the West Indies—so they could then make their way up to Ipswich Dock. The channel was not deep enough to allow passage to fully laden vessels. In severe winters the ships would be preceded by small barges manned by men carrying rammer-headed poles with which to break the ice. Every July the spritsail barges still come to Butterman's Bay for the Pin Mill barge race in which they race, out to sea and up the River Stour before finishing at the Pin Mill hard. It is a short, pleasant walk from Clamp House—the name comes from the peat which was cut and clamped (stacked) here—to Pin Mill through the woods by the river where the old barges are tied up. Some are used as dwellings or artists' studios. Pin Mill (pin from pynd or pond) is the best known and loved sailing spot along the east coast, where generations of sailors and smugglers from home and abroad have swapped yarns and indulged in drinking, dancing and merrymaking in the Butt and Oyster. The field opposite the pub was once used for archery practice and the inn may have taken its name from the butts on the field.

Boat building and barge repairing has been the life blood of Pin Mill, and Kings are still the boat builders. They built the *Selina King* for Arthur Ransome, the children's author, best known for his book, *Swallows and Amazons*. His great-grandfather, John Atkinson Ransome, founded the Ipswich engineering firm of Ransome and Rapier. In 1935 Arthur Ransome moved from the Lake District to Suffolk so that he could sail at Pin Mill. When he asked the removal man if he would like to stay overnight, the man declined with the remark, "No thank you sir, I'd best be getting back to England."

Ransome first lived at Broke Hall, Levington, and then at Harkstead Hall before returning to the Lake District. Whilst in Suffolk he wrote *Secret Waters*, a story set in Essex marshland, *The Big Six* a picture of life on the Norfolk Broads, and *We Didn't Mean to Go to Sea*, a story based on four children staying at Alma Cottage, Pin Mill, accidentally stranded on a seven-ton cutter on which they sailed, with many adventures, across the Channel to Flushing. Arthur Ransome was awarded the Carnegie medal in 1936 for the best children's book of the year.

18

The Butt and Oyster public house at Pin Mill.

Another Pin Mill author was E Arnot Robertson, whose book, *Ordinary Families*, published in 1933, was based in Pin Mill.

Of all the hards that run into the River Orwell, some with exotic names such as Slumpy Lane, Cat House or Red Gate, the best known is Pin Mill. At one time half a dozen or more barges would rest their flat bottoms on the hard to be repaired. In earlier times it was easier to travel between villages by boat, rowing from one hard to the next, than doing the journey on foot or horseback. Passengers would require a pair of paukes or poits, wooden boards strapped to their feet, to prevent them sinking into the soft mud.

In 1338 the bailiffs of Ipswich claimed the right of maritime jurisdiction from Edward III, to administer the customary law of the sea, called the Admiralty, from the hards to all passing mariners. Because of the continuous passage of ships, such matters had to be dealt with swiftly. The Admiralty were the fore-runners of the present harbour boards; they dealt with dredging, moorings and fishing rights and levied anchorage dues known as the knowledge penny.

I picked up the coastal path again behind King's boat yard opposite the Butt and Oyster, and continued by a most pleasant well-worn path by the river in

Masts and spritsails at Pin Mill.

front of Woolverstone Hall to Cat House hard and the resplendent club house of
the famous Royal Harwich Yacht Club. Woolverstone Hall, a large mansion, with
beautiful panoramic views from its vantage point on the hill, was built for
William Berners in 1776. His mother was a descendant of Cromwell; he himself
owned and gave his name to Berners Street in London. He was obsessed with
monkeys and placed monkey statues in prominent positions on his buildings. It
is thought that a monkey saved the life of one of the Berner family, for a monkey
figure was adopted as the family crest with the motto "I escaped the fire."

Named originally as the Eastern Yacht Club, the Royal Harwich Yacht Club
was founded in 1843 at a dinner held in the Three Cups Hotel by the Harwich
Regatta Committee. Its present patron is Prince Philip; former patrons were
Queen Adelaide, Queen Victoria, the Prince Consort, King George V, who was
the club's Commodore for fifteen years when he was Prince of Wales, and King
George VI. Its emblem with a lion rampant has been flown in many parts of the
world but notably at the America's Cup and on polar expeditions. Its original
headquarters was at the Baths and Club Room near the now departed Ordnance
Pier in Harwich. After the war it was realized that there was no attractive
anchorage at Harwich for smaller boats, and it was decided to move to

Woolverstone, where the new club house was opened on 31st May, 1969, by round-the-world yachtsman Robin Knox-Johnston.

On the other side of the concrete roadway is the Cat House, a steep gabled Gothic cottage built in 1793. The north side had a three-light dummy window on which was painted a cat and an hour glass. Traditionally a stuffed white cat was placed in a lighted window as a signal to smugglers that the coast was clear for them to make a run in. I noticed that the present occupiers keep up with tradition by placing a porcelain cat in the window. At present there is no public right of way through Woolverstone Marina and along the coastal path, which formed a carriageway to Woolverstone Hall from the Monkey Lodge. Many notices indicated the land was private and warned trespassers to keep to the foreshore, so I returned and walked up the concrete roadway until, just past the Cat House, I could take the path on the left hand side of the road, on the right of the boundary railings, to the club house and on, almost parallel with the road, to the delightful park, in which there is the fourteenth-century church of Woolverstone. This contains stained-glass windows in memory of the Berner family. From here the footpath is well marked and goes along the top of the field to the right, over the concrete runway and past the Lutyens-designed Woolverstone House and then, after about half a mile, turns right to Freston Tower and ends on the shore.

Freston Tower, originally known as Latymer Tower, is a six-storeyed Tudor brick tower probably built during the sixteenth century by a member of the Latymer family. It has been suggested that it was a quiet retreat for Edmund Latymer or used as a lookout for shipping by smugglers. Between 1772 and 1779 it was an isolation hospital for people with smallpox run by Mr Buck, an Ipswich surgeon.

The nineteenth-century novelist, the Reverend Richard Cobbold, Rector of Wortham, who wrote the novel *Freston Tower*, states that it was built for Ellen Latymer by her father, the Lord of Freston, as a place for her to complete her studies. Poor people came to the ground floor between eight and nine in the morning for Ellen to hear their needs. The first floor was devoted to tapestry until ten o'clock, and on the second floor she sang and practised the lute or lyre until noon. The third floor was reserved for an hour's painting followed by literature reading in her library on the fourth floor until two. Her evenings were occupied by studying the stars from her sixth floor—a pretty busy day! Ellen Latymer married a distant cousin, William, and because this was a very happy marriage it became the custom for newly weds to visit Freston Tower on their wedding day. Richard Cobbold wrote:

> No burgess on his wedding day
> Which falls in whitethorn merry May,
> Shall be happy in house or bower
> Who does not visit Freston Tower.

Because of the strong connection between the Protestants of the Reformation and the House of Latymer, the local Roman Catholic priests plotted to burn down Freston Manor, a square fortified building with a huge portcullis, drawbridge and four towers, surrounded by a moat nearly a hundred feet wide. Abdil Foley is named as the person responsible for burning down the mansion.

I turned my back on Freston Tower and retraced my steps a short distance before taking the path that brought me out opposite the Boot Inn on Freston Hill, from where I proceeded downhill past Monkey Lodge and on to the Strand, the road that runs beside the river.

Stubs of wooden posts in straight lines sticking out of the mud are now the only reminder of the old hards. Immediately below Monkey Lodge was Slumpy Lane wharf and the dock near Freston Tower, from which in 1757 the *Lion*, a thirty-six ton yacht, was sold. Further along the Strand are the remains of Red Gate hard. W. G. Arnott has suggested that this hard was, in medieval times, the south side of Downham Bridge, a place where the Orwell could be crossed at low tide to Pond Hall hard on the opposite shore. This crossing may have been used in Roman times, when it would have linked the Roman road from Colchester to a Roman fort at Walton now submerged beneath the sea off Felixstowe. I first became aware of Red Gate hard or Downham Bridge whilst erecting a hide on the Orwell mud to photograph the many estuary birds that come down from the Arctic to winter here. Dunlins, small streaked birds with grey winter breasts and

Freston Tower; it is said to have been the property of the Latimer family, but this remains a mystery.

black bellies in summer, are the most numerous and together with knots, similar but larger birds, roost in thousands at high tide in the field on the opposite side of the road, waiting for the tide to go out so they can resume feeding off the crustacea within the mud. Redshanks, the noisy ones with red legs, turnstones, oystercatchers, plovers—the list is almost endless if the wildfowl and passage birds are included, particularly those that have been blown off course. This is a bird watchers' paradise with an international reputation. Winter is the time for cormorants, sitting on posts with outstretched wings as they dry out.

"That bird'll never pull that post out of the mud", remarked a woman on a passing bus as she spotted a cormorant, "It's far too big for it."

Summer sees the herons stand motionless, seemingly on tip toe as they stealthily stalk their prey of fish and eels along the river's edge. Queen Elizabeth I once ordered the heronry to be destroyed after the local fishermen had complained of unfair competition, but happily the herons survived.

At the end of the Strand next to Bourne Bridge stands a very ancient hostelry known as the Ostrich. The inn took its name from the landowner's (Sir Edward Coke, Chief Justice of James I and Earl of Leicester) coat of arms, which includes a picture of an ostrich about to swallow an iron horseshoe. This feat was intended to symbolize the Chief Justice's professional capacity to digest the legal difficulties put before him no matter how tough or unpalatable they were. A locally held view is that this part of the Orwell once contained oyster beds and

The Ostrich Inn at Bourn Bridge.

that ostrich is a derivation of oyster reach, but the inn sign with its painted ostrich and horseshoe shows the true derivation.

The new Orwell Bridge makes the north bank of the river easily accessible without having to go through Ipswich—what a blessing. Unfortunately the planner omitted to make a pedestrian access to the bridge from the Strand, but there is a public footpath parallel to the bridge which goes first to Wherstead Church and then to the village, from where the bridge can be approached along the side of the access road.

Wherstead Church, once used as a navigation point, has the best view of the river and has been described as "Superior to anything to be found in Scotland". The Reverend Foster Barham Zincke, chaplain to Queen Victoria, was the incumbent at Wherstead during the last century, when he wrote a history of the parish which was first published as a series of articles in the *Suffolk Chronicle*. The spoliation of the countryside and the need for conservation is thought to be a contemporary problem, but a hundred years ago Zincke was complaining about the destruction of the Wherstead hedgerows, on which he blamed the scarcity of snakes, hedgehogs and toads. He recorded that the purple emperor butterfly, now one of the rarest of British butterflies, was once common in Holbrook Park.

Country folk, then as now, were hunting enthusiasts. One parishioner, listening to the parson's sermon from the porch, spotted a fox leaving its den and overcome with excitement gave the cry "Tally Ho!" and emptied the church

The Orwell Bridge.

of its congregation! On another occasion the gamekeeper pleaded with the squire to prevent the parson from holding a service for fear of disturbing a partridge that had nested close to the church door.

In the churchyard is the grave of Robert Gooding, who died on 27th August, 1618, described on his stone as a salt finer. There had been at least one salt works on the Strand since Domesday, where the sea water was trapped and then allowed to evaporate, a practice that died out with the advent of modern transport, which made it easier and cheaper to bring salt from the Cheshire mines.

Eastern Electricity have their headquarters in the white brick house built in Wherstead park by Sir Jeffrey Wyatville for Sir Robert Harland in 1792. Many notable dignitaries have received hospitality beneath its roof; it was rented by Lord Granville, father of the Secretary of Foreign Affairs in Gladstone's ministry. Granville was accidentally shot by the Duke of Wellington while they were out pheasant shooting—"It was better than hitting the pheasant!" The Duke of York stayed there and Edward Fitzgerald's parents rented the house.

Barely a hundred years ago on 30th October, 1891, Bourne Bridge was widened from thirteen to twenty-seven feet to accommodate the rapidly increasing horsedrawn traffic trotting into Ipswich from the surrounding estates of the gentry. It cost the Ipswich corporation, the county council and a few private contributors £1200 and a celebration dinner at the Ostrich. At the beginning of the century, it is recorded that only one four-wheel carriage, that of Mrs Berner of Woolverstone Hall, drawn by four Suffolk Punches, used the bridge. This was the time when the roadways or rather trackways became very wide as horses and carriages were driven on the verges to avoid the mud, ruts and ridges. A plough was kept in Wherstead Church and a man was employed to plough away the ruts in the road. Broom was purchased by the parish and laid in the mud, and faggots filled up the holes. Quarter carts were then in use. These had their horse shafts placed off-centre to enable the horse to walk along the ridge between two ruts while the wheels avoided them. Cuttings down a hillside appeared naturally as the rain washed away the soft mud churned up by the horses and carriages.

The Orwell Bridge of today is a study in concrete, an aesthetically pleasing engineering masterpiece replacing the old Bourne Bridge as a short cut across the Orwell. Its four-lane carriageway forms part of the Ipswich bypass, which carries heavy traffic from Felixstowe docks to the industrial Midlands and the metropolis. It is four-fifths of a mile long and eighty feet wide, and its more than six-hundred-foot central span, under which the ships pass, is the longest single span of pre-stressed concrete in the United Kingdom. Over a hundred thousand cubic yards of cement were used in the construction, and it has nineteen sets of reinforced concrete piers built upon groups of concrete piles that go into the ground to a depth of 120 feet. It took over three years to build.

# CHAPTER TWO

# The Orwell Bridge to Ramsholt

THERE is no public right of way on the Ordnance Survey map between the Orwell Bridge and the Nacton shore, but a flight of steep steps from the bridge leads to the shore, which continues along the edge of Bridge Wood to Downham Reach. This walk can be hazardous at high tide, especially near the small quay where there is a tidal inlet blocking the way. It is probably better to reach Nacton shore by road and then continue along the public footpath round Broke Hall to reach the Levington Ship—another delightful Suffolk pub.

Margaret Catchpole, the eighteenth-century Suffolk heroine, has always been associated with Nacton, where, as a young girl, she worked in domestic service. Margaret had the reputation of being a very fine horsewoman, but she stole a horse and rode it seventy miles to London in just ten hours, according to the *Ipswich Journal*. She was caught, and brought to trial at Bury St Edmunds Assizes, convicted of horse stealing and sentenced to death, which was commuted to seven years' transportation to Australia. Whilst awaiting transportation in an Ipswich jail she escaped but was recaptured and resentenced, this time to life. She arrived in Australia in 1801 on the convict ship *Nile*, and was assigned as a domestic to Captain Palmer at Woolloomooloo. Margaret then became a farm overseer and midwife, and helped the settlers to farm the fertile Hawkesbury Plain near Sydney. She became a very respected member of the community and was completely pardoned in 1814. She died unmarried in 1819. Her death certificate reads:

> Margaret Catchpole, aged 58 years, came prisoner in the Ship Nile in the year 1801, died May 13, was buried May 14 1819, By me Henry Fulton

She is buried at St Peter's Church, Richmond; the exact location of her grave is not known, but it is assumed to be next to the Dight family vault as she worked for this family in her latter years.

A Suffolk parson, Richard Cobbold, whose mother employed Margaret Catchpole for a while, wrote a romantic novel about Margaret which he declared was her biography, but many of his facts were incorrect, including the year she was born. This has now been accepted as 1762, not 1773 as recorded by Cobbold. In his novel a preventive officer, Lieutenant Edward Barry, falls in love with

**Opposite:** The figurehead of the *Shannon*. It is now at Shrubland Hall, Coddenham.

Margaret but his love is not reciprocated as Margaret has fallen for smuggler Will Laud. Edward Barry goes to Australia where, according to Cobbold, he eventually meets Margaret again and they marry; the book has a happy ending.

Will Laud had many scrapes with the law, eventually being shot by the preventive officer Edward Barry and his body taken to the Ship Inn at Orford. When, Margaret was told that Will Laud was hiding in London she was tempted to steal a horse. Since it is now believed that Laud was a fictitious figure, why then did Margaret risk death to steal a horse and ride to London? Surely only a woman desperately in love would do this.

Broke Hall at Nacton is red brick and castellated, and in spring is set in a sea of daffodils. The Hall originates from the middle of the sixteenth century, but its present appearance belongs to the eighteenth century. Sir Philip Bowes Vere Broke was born here in 1776. He joined the Royal Navy when he was sixteen and served under Nelson before taking command of Her Majesty's ship *Shannon*, in which he captured the American frigate *Chesapeake*, with forty English sailors aboard, in the war against the United States (1812–14).

At that time the Royal Navy, showing scant respect for US territorial waters,

Broke Hall, Nacton, the home of Admiral Sir Philip Bowes Vere Broke, Commander of the *Shannon*.

stopped and searched American ships suspected of breaking the English blockade of France. Because of the inhumane conditions in the English ships many sailors deserted to the Americans. Officially it was these English sailors the Navy wished to recover, but in doing so they also captured six thousand Americans and impressed them into the Royal Navy. The United States proved a difficult adversary for the arrogant English, who suffered many reverses in this war until 1st June, 1813, when the American frigate *Chesapeake* sailed out of Boston harbour to be defeated by the *Shannon*.

Broke had received severe head injuries from a musket butt, and a slash from a cutlass exposed three inches of his brain. The American captain was mortally wounded but survived in agony for four days, all the time imploring his crew, "not to give up the Ship!" Ninety sailors from both sides died in the engagement; another 128 were wounded.

Broke became a popular hero, as he had reversed the ill fortune of the British Navy in the American war. Nicknamed "Brave Broke" he returned to England in triumph and was knighted in 1815, but his brain had been irreparably damaged and he died undergoing surgery in 1841. Lord Thurlow in 1813 wrote:

> And taught by Broke, Britannia now may view
> What her brave Suffolk to her foes can do.

His brother, Major General Sir Charles Broke, was born in 1779 and joined the army when he was seventeen. He saw action in the Peninsular war against the French, and the Duke of Wellington made him his quartermaster in the middle of the Battle of Waterloo. Both men are buried in Nacton church; the Broke family moved away from the estate in 1945.

Just round the corner from Broke Hall stands Orwell Park. The first view is of towering and decorative iron gates leading to two hundred acres of beautiful parkland reaching down to the river. The original building was the home of Admiral Edwards Vernon. In the Navy he was known as Old Grog because of the grogram material from which his boatcloak was made. To reduce the incidence of drunkenness amongst his men Vernon ordered that the rum ration (one pint a day for men and half a pint for boys) was to be diluted with a quart of water and issued twice daily—diluted rum will not keep and could not therefore be saved for a party. This watered-down liquid became known as "grog", after the Admiral's nick-name, and the word "groggy", the resulting physiological effects of the rum, entered our language. The issue of rum to the Navy was discontinued in 1970.

His most famous naval engagement was against the Spanish in 1739, when he sailed to the West Indies with instructions to burn the Spanish ships he found lingering in the Spanish ports. With only six ships and against all odds, he captured the well-fortified town of Porto Bello in Panama from the guarda-costas, whose task was to prevent smuggling although more often they pillaged

English ships like pirates. He was one of the first Admirals to realize the necessity of exercising his officers in naval manoeuvres and the men in gun drill. On the death of the Admiral, Orwell Park passed to his nephew, Viscount Orwell, who rebuilt it and surrounded it with the large park. As Earl of Shipbroke he died in 1783 and the estate passed to another nephew, John Vernon, whose daughter married Sir Robert Harland. In 1847 the estate was sold to George Tomline, whose grandfather, the Reverend George Pretyman, 1750–1827, was born in Bury St Edmunds. He became both the Bishop of Winchester and also the Bishop of Lincoln. While he was at Lincoln a friend of the Bishop's, Marmaduke Tomline, left his estates to the Bishop, who changed his name from Pretyman to Tomline, although most of his descendants retained the name of Pretyman. George Tomline was unmarried and the last of the family to retain the name of Tomline. Colonel Tomline was born in 1813, educated at Eton, became a Member of Parliament and held the rank of Colonel in the North Lincolnshire Militia. He was, in his time, described as one of the two most intelligent men in the country, the other being Gladstone. Tomline was also very rich. He rebuilt Orwell Park House in 1854 choosing the most grandiose plan his architect could devise. It was customary in those days for architects to submit to their clients a number of plans, some of which were extravagantly expensive, just to show they were capable of designing another Versailles given the opportunity. Needless to say few of the most expensive plans were chosen but Tomline did just that for Orwell Park House. It is now occupied by a preparatory school.

Tomline was a keen astronomer and added an observatory which is a replica of the Salute church in Venice. There are 111 steps to the telescope in the dome, which his astronomer, who lived in the village, was required to climb while Tomline took the lift. He was an eccentric and moved the village of Nacton to the other side of the hill to avoid seeing "a blot on the landscape". The villagers benefited by having modern brick dwellings, but Tomline is supposed to have instructed that the main door should be put at the side of the houses to prevent the women gossiping to their neighbours across the road, and to stop them staring at him as he passed in his carriage. Tomline also purchased Marshal Soult's (Napoleon's Chief of Staff at Waterloo) collection of pictures, which had been stolen from places all over Europe during the Napoleonic wars.

Tomline is best remembered for his two great public works that led to the rapid development of Victorian Felixstowe. He built a railway from Ipswich to Felixstowe, which was opened on 1st May, 1877, and he built the Felixstowe Dock, which was completed in 1886 when the first ship, the *Crathie*, entered to unload its coal. By 1961 the development of efficient cargo handling techniques made Felixstowe the most efficient port in Europe and it is now the largest container handling port in England. The docks continue to expand and will soon reach upstream as far as Fagbury Point, much to the detriment of the wader birds which feed here.

The observatory attached to Orwell Park House was built after the style of the Salute church in Venice by Colonel Tomline.

Colonel Tomline's telescope.

I continued my walk from the Nacton shore to the Port of Felixstowe along the public footpath, which took me round the edge of the Broke Hall estate and up to another pleasant pub—the Levington Ship. According to the author, Richard Cobbold, Levington was the first village on the Orwell celebrated for the cultivation of the rose, encouraged by Hugh Fastolf the Lord of the Manor of Levington Hall. Appropriately Fisons, the fertilizer firm, established their horticultural research station here, having discovered the value of the local crag as a fertilizer.

From the Ship, I walked down the hill and took a short concrete road along the sea wall to Levington Marina. Here the path continues through the wood opposite the old light vessel, now used as a sailing club, past a picturesque trout farm divided from the estuary by the sea wall, and then round the highly cultivated Trimley Marshes to Fagbury Point, meeting the Port of Felixstowe at the junction of Walter and Parker avenues. I continued through the dock area to Landguard Common.

Landguard Fort, declared an Ancient Monument in 1961, is at the southerly tip of Felixstowe beach next to the dock and once guarded the entrance to Harwich harbour. There has been a fortification on Langer Common since the time of Henry VIII, then consisting mostly of earthworks and bastions. Pirate ships, Dunkirkers sailing out of Dunkirk, were partly responsible for the need to strengthen the east coast defences, and a new fort was built at Landguard between 1624 and 1626. It was a handsome square fortification complete with drawbridge, portcullis and bastion at each corner. The governor's house was a resplendent red brick building which matched the double row of red brick barracks on either side of the parade ground. The fort was replaced between 1745 and 1751 on a new site nearer to the river. This one was built in the shape of a pentagon, again with a bastion at each corner and the governor's residence, chapel and barracks placed centrally. It was often garrisoned by a company of Invalids, soldiers who had been wounded in battle and were no longer fit for active service. The fort must have been a pleasant place in which to live. There were beautiful gardens with fruit trees, mainly fig, a tall tamarisk tree and fountains splashing into goldfish pools, while golden plovers, snipe and wildfowl inhabited the Common amongst a plethora of wild flowers.

The notorious Captain Philip Thicknesse (1719–92), having purchased a commission making him the Governor of Landguard Fort, and also known as Lieutenant Gallstones, come to Felixstowe in 1753. He commissioned Thomas Gainsborough to make a painting of the fort. It was Gainsborough's first landscape painting, for which he received fifteen guineas and a violin.

Between 1872 and 1875 the interior of the fort was altered to the semi-circular arrangement of barrack blocks which exists today. The caponier, a covered passage across the outside defensive ditch, with its quarter-sphere bomb-proof shelter was also added to the outside south wall. Further defences were built outside the perimeter of the curtain walls of the fort, left and right batteries, which were armed with heavy guns during both world wars. Ornithologists of the Landguard Bird Ringing group now occupy part of the fort. They record the birds on passage by capturing them in nets hung vertically between posts. The name of the species, its weight, length and wing span are recorded and a ring is placed around its leg for future identification before the bird is released to continue its journey. Floodlights from the adjacent docks attract many of the migratory birds to the land and hence the Landguard bird ringing station is in a very strategic position. A firecrest, a black redstart and a blackcap were just three of the birds I saw ringed during my fascinating dawn vigil at the fort.

In 1667, the year the Dutch ceded New York to the English, the Dutch fleet attacked the Thames and the Medway towns and then turned its attention to Landguard Fort. On 30th June they arrived off Harwich and next day fifty men of war, with their attendant vessels, sailed to attack the fort. The wind was not in their favour so they continued on a northerly course towards Orfordness,

A bird in the hand: this blackcap has had its vital statistics recorded and is now ready to be released back into the wild.

causing a Suffolk Militia regiment to be deployed north of the river Deben. On 2nd July the fleet returned on a southerly course, followed along the cliff tops by the Suffolk Militia commanded by Sir Philip Parker. Four Dutch ships detached from the main fleet attacked and successfully kept the Militia at Bawdsey until late in the afternoon, when the ebbing tide forced the ships to withdraw.

33

Earlier the main fleet anchored off Felixstowe and ferried sixteen hundred men to the shore, landing them on the south side of Cobbold's point, near Felixstowe College. Five hundred soldiers, including pikemen, were deployed to hold the beach head and the cliff tops, while the remainder of the force, including four hundred sailors, marched to Landguard led by the renegade Englishman Colonel Dolman.

The Dutch fleet attempted to bombard the fort at half past two in the afternoon, but low water over the sand shoals made them ineffective. After many sorties the Dutch decided that the fort was impenetrable and retreated to their beachhead where, fortunately for them, Dutch troops had kept the Suffolk Militia at bay, permitting a successful withdrawal before midnight.

Out on Landguard Common the sea holly or sea thistle flourishes between the pebbles in a windswept, hostile environment sometimes covered by the encroaching sea. This tough, resilient little plant was chosen as their emblem by the Suffolk Artillery Militia, formed in 1853. The deep roots of the sea holly were once used as a cure-all medicine. According to the *English Physician Enlarged*, first published in 1653, sea holly roots were used to open obstructions of the spleen and liver, to cure yellow jaundice, dropsy, wind and colic as well as defects of the kidney and pulmonary diseases and proved excellent against the French pox. If that were not enough it was in demand as an aphrodisiac! One important use, until recently, was to make the roots into sweets known as eringoes, a speciality of Colchester and enjoyed by Shakespeare. Falstaff in *The Merry Wives of Windsor* declares:

A box of eringoes. (Courtesy of Colchester museum)

Let the sky rain potatoes;
Let it thunder to the tune of greensleeves,
Hail kissing comfits and snow eringoes . . .

In 1761 Princess Charlotte, when on her way from Harwich to marry George III, was presented with a box of them. Robert Buxton, a Mayor of Colchester, was the first person to make eringoes. The roots were taken from a depth of six feet then peeled and boiled to make them tender, before being immersed in cold water for several days. The pith was removed and the roots spread out and cut into strips and twisted together to resemble a barley sugar stick. A 1633 recipe says they were then soaked in very strong sugar syrup to which was added an egg white, a little orange flower water and drops of rose and cinnamon "with a grain of muske". Finally the eringoes were dried in front of the fire on trays of plaited cane.

The rare sea kale grows profusely on Landguard Common, as does the sea pea. The blanched root of the sea kale was once an important vegetable. Called sickels, they were very tasty when fried in breadcrumbs and sprinkled with lemon juice or served on toast with lashings of butter, and could be boiled and eaten like asparagus. The Common has since 1979 been a nature reserve managed by the Suffolk Trust for Nature Conservation. Its rare wildlife, including a colony of rare breeding little terns amongst the shingle, makes it a Site of Special Scientific Interest, spoiled a little by human encroachment, including litter on the beach.

On the outskirts of modern Felixstowe between holiday caravans and rows of tightly packed beach huts, stands a solitary Martello tower on Wireless Green, once used as a naval telegraphy station communicating with destroyers operating from Harwich. It is now a coastguard station and one of the eleven remaining from eighteen towers built to defend the Suffolk coast against French invasion during the Napoleonic wars.

The towers were named after a Corsican watch tower at Mortella Point, which had proved to be very resistant to attack by the Royal Navy. When Napoleon set his sights on invading England, with his army camped at Boulogne, the military decided to construct the Martello towers. Work commenced on the Suffolk towers in 1808 after the French had been defeated at Trafalgar in 1805. It was thought at the time that the French might land on the flat lands of East Anglia and then march south towards London.

The Suffolk towers are egg-shaped with the narrower end having the thickest wall facing the sea. Each tower required about three quarters of a million yellow bricks, specially made in London, set in a mortar of lime ash and hot tallow that dried as hard as iron. The single entrance door was placed high above ground level and reached by a removable rope ladder. A stairway built into the walls led to the roof, which supported a gun battery. Its purpose was to provide concentrated fire on ships and to repel enemy landings. The towers, although capable of withstanding a long siege, were never used in anger; being difficult to demolish, they now form part of our military defence heritage along the east coast, dating from Roman times to the concrete gun emplacements and tank traps of the Second World war.

The martello tower at Felixstowe Ferry.

Felixstowe perpetuates the memory of Bishop Felix, who arrived in East Anglia from Burgundy in the reign of King Sigebert in the seventh century to convert the East Angles to Christianity. He must have done a good job, for the historian Bede records:

> Felix reaped a rich harvest of believers and delivered the entire province from its age old wickedness and infelicity.

The name Felixstowe may also have come from Fileth Stowe meaning a place where trees have been felled.

Charles Manning's Amusement Arcade begins a mile or so along the Felixstowe front. Travelling circuses were the first to entertain the public here towards the end of the last century. Before the 1939 war people came here to see the bears, monkeys and lions owned by the famous holiday camp veteran, Billy Butlin. The lions were too old or tired to be dangerous, but a terrified baboon which had escaped and sought refuge in the ladies' toilet caused a minor sensation. After the war Butlin gave his friend, Charles Manning, the opportunity to run the fairground.

As well as the garish fun fairs, flickering lights and dodgem cars, Felixstowe promenade has the prim boarding houses and inviting cafes, excited children disposing of candy floss, hot dogs, chips and ice cream, sand castles and sun bathers. It was not always like this. In 1854 Humble Gumble, who, it has been suggested, was Bishop Harvey Goodwin of Cambridge University, came this way and records travelling by train from Cambridge to Felixstowe for a fare of five shillings and then taking the steamer, *The Cardinal Wolsey*, to Harwich, from where he crossed to Landguard on a ferry for a further five shillings.

At this time visitors came from Ipswich in horsedrawn buses, often in convoy, and the buses were invariably overloaded to such an extent that the horses couldn't or wouldn't move. The journey took about three and a half hours.

Sea bathers dressed themselves in blue serge suits with short legs and sleeves and hired a bathing hut at a shilling each allowing them privacy while bathing. Unlike most bathing huts of the time, which were pulled from the water by a horse, those at Felixstowe were winched up using a cable and windlass, controlled with a long hand spike by the proprietor. Humble Gumble described the few beach huts located near Cobbold's Point as small wooden boxes with a door at one end, a window opening to the sea and a wooden bench running round the inside. They were hired by the less well-off, who sat eating whelks and fish and drinking beer while watching the sea roll in. Donkey rides were popular and beachcombing, as now, was a favourite pastime, particularly amongst young girls, who hoped to find amber or colourful stones, such as agate or cornelian—a beautiful mineral composed of silica.

The modern Edwardian seaside resort developed rapidly once Colonel Tomline had brought the railway to Felixstowe. The pier was opened in 1905. It was originally three-quarters of a mile long, the second longest in the country, Southend pier being a mile long. Electric carriages carried passengers at a penny a ride and steamers called there on their way between London and Yarmouth. The pavilion has been demolished to make way for a sport and leisure complex but the Spa pavilion, bombed in 1941 and re-opened in 1950, still provides a venue for sea-side entertainment. The gardens are delightful, overlooked by the majestic building that was once the Felix Hotel.

The promenade runs out by the Fludyer Hotel, which bears the name of the family who purchased the fisherman's cottage on Cobbold Point—formerly the home of the wife of the Landguard Fort Governor, Philip Thicknesse, who developed it into an elegant residence. When Mr Cobbold built the present mansion on the site, now part of Felixstowe College, Cottage Point became Cobbold's Point.

As the tide was out I clambered over the rocks of Cobbold's Point and made my way past more beach huts until I ascended the cliff in front of Brackenbury Barracks. Brackenbury Fort was built on this site during the First World War. A railway line specially constructed from Felixstowe station brought the heavy guns to the fort, but it is understood that they were never fired with a full charge for fear of bringing down the crumbling cliffs. The fort has gone now, as has that other ancient fort before it, Walton Castle, the remaining rubble of which lies two or three hundred yards out to sea. It was a Norman castle built and owned by the Barons Bigod, Earls of Norfolk, until Henry II confiscated and eventually destroyed it after the baronial revolt of 1173, the year in which his new castle at Orford was ready for him. I descended onto the edge of the golf course and from that Martello Tower I caught my first and best view of Bawdsey Manor, its towers protruding above the trees on the opposite bank of the Deben. It must have been near this point that the young Cuthbert Quilter, sitting on the back of his grandfather's farm cart, looked across to the promontory at Bawdsey and vowed that if he made a fortune he would build his castle here. He did just that.

Cuthbert Quilter was born in 1841 in the City of London, where he made his fortune as a stockbroker with the firm of Quilter, Balfour and Company and also made money in several business enterprises. When he was thirty-two he moved from Surrey to Suffolk to build his manor. The building is an architectural hotch potch. A pseudo-Elizabethan red tower block was the earliest part of the building, then came the oriental white tower, which was the children's wing, with a lift that never worked. These towers were joined by a mock Tudor front. Particularly impressive is the dark panelling of the main hall, used as the officers' dining hall, and the bright, sunlit orangery, which has delightful views looking out across the Deben estuary. Sir Cuthbert Quilter knew what he was about. Local tradition states that every time Sir Cuthbert made a million he added another tower. There are nine towers in all.

There was a large staff which included a butler, footman, valet, hall boy, four kitchen staff including the cook, six housemaids, fourteen gardeners and five game keepers. Staff were strictly disciplined, as were the children, who went in awe of cook and Lady Quilter's personal maid. Every morning the family and staff would gather in the billiard room for prayers. The children had their respective kneeling positions on the hard oak steps beneath the buttoned leather seats. When the short service was over the family would chat before going down to breakfast. This was an enormous affair. Bowls of porridge were kept on rows of copper-plated warmers heated by methylated spirit burners. This was followed by dishes of eggs, bacon, sausages, kidneys, kedgeree and a cold table consisting of a Suffolk ham, tongue and poultry. The meal was completed with toast and hot scones accompanied by tea or coffee served from huge silver pots. Newspapers were placed on a separate table after the creases had been ironed out!

The mock Tudor front of Bawdsey Manor.

The Kaiser is reputed to have stayed at Bawdsey Manor before the First World War and promised that his zeppelins would not bomb the manor if war was declared, but a zeppelin did appear one day over Bruisyard. An excited farm hand, encouraged by his children who said, "Go on Dad, you cannot miss that one", took a pot shot at it with his twelve bore at the precise moment it was hit by fire from attacking aircraft. To the farm hand's delight the zeppelin caught fire and crashed. He reckoned it was the highest cock pheasant he had ever shot in Suffolk!

Cuthbert Quilter became the Liberal MP for South Suffolk in 1885. He was an advocate of ensuring purity in food, including beer, which he wanted made solely from barley, malt and hops, and introduced a Bill into Parliament for "The better securing the Purity of Beer". It didn't get further than its first reading. He also opened, for a short time, a small brewery in nearby Melton in which to brew his pure ale. Ironically he also took part in the movement that led to the abolition of cottage brewing licences, and home brewing has only very recently become legal again. Perhaps he thought it was the impurities in the beer that caused drunkenness or he knew that added sugar increased the alcohol content when fermented!

Lady Quilter also took an interest in philanthropic work and invited the girls from the East End Working Girls' Clubs to spend their holiday at Bawdsey. When a groundsman confronted one of the girls bathing in the nude, she retorted:

If you can see anything 'ere God ain't made, you can throw your cap at it!

Cuthbert Quilter was made a baronet in 1906 just five years before he died in 1911 aged seventy. It was the end of an era in which there was great wealth and great poverty. Everyone knew their place in society, the Governor was not addressed unless he opened the conversation first, and every respect was given to his position. He was omnipotent but, on the whole, his employees could lead a strict but satisfying existence—unless they went poaching, which was an unpardonable offence.

In 1936 the manor was sold to the Air Ministry and it remained an RAF station until 1990. It was here that Sir Robert Watson-Watt developed radar, which enabled our fighter pilots to detect enemy aircraft in the dark. Watson-Watt started his work at Orfordness but was required to find new premises; the Air Ministry was able to purchase Bawdsey Manor for the meagre sum of £24,000. In July, 1959, the Duchess of Gloucester unveiled a plaque which reads:

In the year 1936 at Bawdsey Manor
Robert Watson-Watt
and his team of scientists developed
the first air defence radar warning station.
The results achieved by these pioneers played
a vital part in the successful outcome of
the Battle of Britain in 1940.

RAF Bawdsey became an operational radar station at the beginning of the Second World War, first tracking enemy aircraft approaching the east coast and alerting the British fighters to attack, giving them the enemy position, course and speed—a system which was instrumental in winning the Battle of Britain. Later they were engaged in plotting the Allied bombing forces flying out to attack Germany, and after the war they plotted Russian aircraft over the North Sea as they tried to probe and test our air defences. This last task has now been taken over by the Early Warning System and RAF Bawdsey ceased operations in March 1975. It opened again in 1979, with Bloodhound missiles parked in the grounds until it closed as an RAF station in 1990.

Felixstowe Ferry has real character bred from the necessity of earning a living from the hostile environment of the sea. It contrasts sharply with the past opulence of Bawdsey Manor on one side and the frivolous gaiety of Felixstowe's seaside resort on the other. Here is a small, hard-working community wresting a living from the sea either by building and repairing small boats, or sailing in them to catch fish. Fresh cod, plaice, shrimps, lobsters and crabs can be bought from the stalls along the shingle beach.

Sir Cuthbert Quilter installed a steam powered chain ferry across the river in 1894 and the boats, Lady Beatrice and Lady Quilter, pulled themselves across the river with the chains laid on the river bed. The ferries were wide enough to accommodate a coach and four horses. The chain ferry remained operational until 1931 and was run by Charles Brinkley. He had lost his right hand when a gun he was holding exploded; his hand was replaced with a hook. Watson-Watt, who travelled frequently on the ferry, named a piece of radar apparatus the Brinkley Hook, in honour of this well-liked boatman.

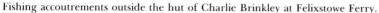

Fishing accoutrements outside the hut of Charlie Brinkley at Felixstowe Ferry.

Those, like me, exploring the length of the Suffolk coast are required to walk the sea walls along the Deben estuary to Woodbridge, the nicest town in East Anglia, as the ferry is not now readily available.

The way out of Felixstowe Ferry is a continuation of the path along the sea edge of the golf course, passing both Martello towers before crossing the road to continue on the sea wall, starting at the far side of the car park, along the Deben estuary. As I rested on a stile, a weasel crept beneath me, gave an inquisitive look and went, happily unperturbed, about its business. In the adjoining field a flock of Canada geese were pairing off and making quite a noise about it. It seems that this corner of Suffolk has been famous for its geese since the Anglo-Saxons first gave the name Goseford—the ford haunted by geese—to the creeks and inlets of the Deben estuary. Goseford included the nearby Anglo-Saxon settlements of Falkenham, Kirton, possibly Woodbridge, Alderton and Bawdsey. Goseford and the Deben estuary became a medieval port, and in 1338 King Edward III waited for his fleet to assemble at King's Fleet. They sailed with a large complement of men to defeat the French off Sluys in 1340. Calais was captured in 1347 and Goseford was required to supply the town with food and beer. Ships sailed from Goseford carrying pilgrims in the Middle Ages to the shrine of St James the Apostle at Compostela in Spain.

In early spring I made a detour from the coastal path to walk along the King's Fleet to Falkenham, originally an Anglo-Saxon settlement. A number of wheatears accompanied me, flitting from one post to the next but keeping just ahead. There is little now at Falkenham except peace, tranquillity and the church. It is one of the few churches dedicated to St Ethelbert, the Anglo-Saxon king who, according to legend, fell in love with the daughter of his overlord king—Offa of Mercia—who ordered his head to be severed in AD 794, presumably to cool his passions! George Roddam and his wife Mary are buried in the churchyard. He was naval physician to King George IV. His wife bequeathed £300, the interest from which was distributed at Christmas for coal and blankets, and the custom still continues for a few parishioners.

On the opposite bank of the Deben, Ramsholt Church stands out as a landmark. It is reputed to have an oval tower. It certainly looks oval, but I am assured it is an optical illusion created by the buttresses, as it is really round. In front of the church is a picturesque quay, at the end of which is the delightfully remote Ramsholt Arms.

Above Kirton Creek the sea wall has been breached, making further progress along it impossible, although the red dots of the Ordnance Survey footpath optimistically continue across the water. From the small dock in Kirton Creek, where a hundred years ago barges distributed the locally made bricks, and ferries plied across the river to Ramsholt and Shottisham, I made my way inland along a farm track first to Hemley Church and then along the road to the one at Newbourn, where the giant brothers George and Meadows Page are buried. George was seven foot, seven inches tall and Meadows was two inches shorter. They were both farm labourers until one day in 1868 they visited Samuel Whiting's Easter fair at Woodbridge. In one of the sideshows, a tall man invited the public to take a guinea from his hand held above his head; the brothers succeeded and were invited by Whiting to join the fair. They accepted. George fell in love with a very small woman, Kat Ewing, who made wax dolls for her father, associated with Madame Tussaud. When George died in 1870, she married Meadows and opened a small shop in Newbourn. George's grave is the third on the left coming out of the church and bears the inscription:

> The deceased was exhibited in most towns in England, but his best exhibition was with his blessed Redeemer.

Each year hundreds of tons of cherry tomatoes, lettuce, celery and other salad crops are grown under acres of glass at Newbourn, and delivered to local supermarkets and major stores throughout the country. This horticultural interest was started in 1934 by the Land Settlement Association, set up to find work for unemployed industrial workers. They purchased two hundred acres of land at Newbourn, on which they erected fifty houses. The first twenty trainees were unemployed Geordies from the Durham coalfields, who were given 3s 6d a week pocket money during their six month training period, after which they and their families were allocated a smallholding, anything from ten acres for open horticulture with pigs and poultry, down to three acre sites for intensive cultivation under glass. The settlement, under an estate manager, was responsible for providing the livestock, seed, feeding stuff, hired machinery, marketing facilities and, thankfully for the tenants, bookkeeping.

When war broke out in 1939 new tenants were expected to have had previous agricultural experience and around £300 capital before taking up a tenancy. This proved to be an attractive proposition for local agricultural workers. After the war when the Ministry of Agriculture acquired the estate, with the Land Settlement acting as their agents, the terms of tenancy were increased to five years' experience, twenty-five per cent of the working capital of £560 plus sufficient money to live on for a year.

By 1955 the Settlement was self-supporting but in 1983 the Ministry of Agriculture dropped a bombshell by abolishing the Land Settlement Association. Ten of the forty Newbourn growers agreed to pool their resources in a co-operative—Newbourn Growers Ltd. Each member put up an initial interest-free loan of £1,500 and promised to commit their salad crops to the co-operative for five years. Newbourn Growers are now part of a larger co-operative, Home Salads Ltd, which includes a hundred growers from Ardleigh near Colchester, Fen Drayton Growers at Cambridge and Fulney Growers in Lincolnshire.

The Fox pub in Newbourn is said to be constructed from ship's timbers, as the bolt holes remain. From here I wandered back to the river at Waldringfield

Falkenham church.

Ramsholt church, whose tower looks oval but is round.

along narrow twisting country lanes, their high banks covered with the white flowers of cow parsley. Waldringfield is an idyllic hamlet favoured by weekend sailing enthusiasts who revive themselves after their exertions at the Maybush, a popular inn. The rustic charm of this quiet village was interrupted when a cement works was built in 1872. Waldringfield then became an industrial inferno. Mud dug from the Deben was mixed with chalk brought by barge from the Thames and baked in kilns to make cement. Two men filled a small barge with mud using scuppets—wooden shovels with steel tips—and dug out twenty-five tons in two and a half hours. On shore the mud, chalk and water were mixed to the right consistency to form a slurry. The mud was "tasted" for grittiness and the correct amount of chalk was added. The slurry was left to settle in tanks, the surplus water drawn off and the precipitated mixture hardened sufficiently to be dug out and placed on the floors of drying rooms. The dried and hardened clay chalk mixture was then loaded into large bottle-shaped kilns between layers of coke and furnace refuse brought by barge from the Deptford gas works. The kilns were fired for several days; the flames leaping out of the top could be seen for miles across the countryside. The resulting clinker, now cement, was ground into a powder, bagged up and loaded on barges and delivered to customers. Workers started at 6 am, which for many meant starting from their outlying villages at 4 am. If they were late they were fined "two pence worth of sleep". The hard, dusty work finished at 5 30 pm but the wages were good for the times, averaging twenty-five shillings a week. In 1907 a new rotary kiln was invented and the Waldringfield cement works became redundant. The pier, where the barges tied up, was demolished, as were three chimneys and twelve kilns. Five years later, in 1912, a modern works opened at Claydon. Country quiet returned to Waldringfield.

Every schoolboy who has studied physics will be familiar with Bragg's Law but they are unlikely to know that Sir Lawrence Bragg, its originator and world famous scientist, lived at Quietways in Waldringfield. He was warm, friendly and kind and when we met our conversation even touched on the best way to make a cup of tea! The secret, taught to him by Joe Lyons himself, is to infuse the tea leaves very slowly, adding boiling water to the tea a little at a time.

Sir Lawrence Bragg was born in Adelaide, Australia, in 1890 and was a graduate of Trinity College, Cambridge. During the 1914–18 war he earned the Military Cross for devising a scheme using the speed of sound to locate the enemy guns. He and his father, Sir William Bragg, were joint winners of the Nobel Prize for their investigations into the structure of crystals using X-rays—a method now used to unravel the structure of the most complex molecules, especially in medical and cancer research. He was a member of the Waldring-field Sailing Club, loved bird watching, particularly at Minsmere, and was dedicated to the scientific education of young people. He was knighted in 1941 and became Companion of Honour in 1967. He died in 1983 aged eighty-one.

The late Sir Lawrence Bragg.

A breach in the wall north of Waldringfield caused me to take to the country lanes again to reach Martlesham Creek, where a short footpath through a copse at the head of the creek led me down to the water's edge and a footpath to Kyson Point and the Woodbridge marina, presided over by its famous and picturesque tide mill.

The restored Woodbridge Tide Mill, which dates from 1793, proudly displaying its gleaming white weatherboarding surmounted by its orange pantile roof, is the last tide mill in England whose machinery is still capable of grinding corn. The mill was worked by the incoming tide filling the mill pool, the water being retained behind sluice gates as the tide receded. The pressure of the water within the pool kept the sluices shut. The water was then diverted through the race to turn the wheel after the tide had gone out; the mill could be worked for two hours either side of low tide during which time it could grind about four hundredweight of corn. Its working life came to an end in 1957 when the square oak shaft of the water wheel broke, and the mill pool became part of the yachting marina.

Woodbridge Tide Mill.

The mill deteriorated rapidly, but in 1968 Mrs Jean Gardner of Gifford's Hall, Wickhambrook, purchased the mill and gave it to the Woodbridge Tide Mill Trust who restored it at a cost of £70,000. The mill was opened to the public in 1973 although it still required a tidal pool to operate it. Mr Peter Wyllie worked ceaselessly throughout his retirement to see the mill working again but unfortunately died five years before his dream came to fruition. Wyllie's Pool is a fitting reminder of his dedication. He was also honoured by the Woodbridge Town Council with the Fellowship Cup for outstanding service to the community.

Woodbridge is my favourite country town and an ideal place from which to start an exploration of the Suffolk coast, particularly as it has a direct rail link with London. The market square, the ancient centre of Woodbridge, lies uphill from the river on Market Hill, where in medieval times an annual fair was held on 23rd October, St Audrey's Day. St Audrey was Queen Ethelreda, born at Exning in Suffolk, the daughter of Anna, King of the East Angles. Her chief claim to fame, apart from building a monastery on the site of the present cathedral at Ely and becoming its abbess, was to marry twice without consummating neither marriage. At St Audrey's Fair they sold necklaces of silk and lace, but these were often of such poor quality that the word tawdry, a corruption of St Audrey, was applied to them.

Woodbridge owes a great deal to Thomas Seckford, the eminent Tudor lawyer. He came from a prominent Suffolk family which was influential at the court of Queen Elizabeth I. He was the Master of requests at the court first established by Cardinal Wolsey for poor men's causes. The court travelled with the Queen on her progress through England and the Master of Court went with her. Seckford also sat on many different commissions and was involved with cases of treason brought against the Roman Catholics. Whether they received a fair hearing from a court whose existence depended on the favour of the Queen can only be guessed. He also dealt with requests for pardons for such crimes as robbery, sheep stealing and piracy. In 1575 Thomas Seckford moved the local Sessions court from Melton to Woodbridge, to what is now known as the Shire Hall. Originally it was an open arcaded market place. Seckford had a room built above the market. A century later stone steps and railings were added and the arcades were bricked in to give the building its present appearance. This three-storeyed building on Market Hill with stone-coped Dutch gable is now used as the administrative offices of the Woodbridge Town Council.

Thomas Seckford is best remembered in Woodbridge for the Seckford Hospital and almshouses endowed with funds raised from investments in Clerkenwell properties. Woodbridge's benefactor died in 1587 and is buried at St Mary's Church, which stands beside the market place next to the Abbey, a Tudor residence built by Seckford and used by his family. It is now the preparatory department of Woodbridge School.

Edward Fitzgerald, the nineteenth-century Woodbridge eccentric, achieved fame with his free translation from the Persian of the *Rubaiyat* of Omar Khayyam. Omar Khayyam was born at Naishapur in Persia about AD 1050, the son of a tent maker, and his poetic work was not appreciated in his own country. Edward Fitzgerald was born of wealthy parents at Bredfield just outside Woodbridge on 31st March, 1809. His father, John Purcell, married his cousin Mary Frances Fitzgerald and in 1818 he adopted the Arms and title of his wife's family. They had eight children of whom Edward was the second eldest. He was educated at the Grammar School at Bury St Edmunds and at Trinity College, Cambridge, where he befriended Thackeray and Tennyson, the latter becoming a lifelong friend. On one occasion the famous poet laureate visited Fitzgerald at Woodbridge and stayed at the Bull Hotel. The landlord, John Grout, was unimpressed by his distinguished guest: "He don't know much about hosses".

Edward Cowell, from Ipswich, introduced Fitzgerald to the Persian language and to the Rubaiyat, a copy of which he had obtained from the Bodleian library at Oxford. Fitzgerald translated it and sent it to *Fraser's Magazine*, where it lingered for a year in the editor's drawer. He then withdrew it and self-published 250 copies. Most of these ended up in the penny bargain box of a London bookseller. Today a copy is valued at more than £10,000. Fitzgerald built the Little Grange, having been evicted from his lodgings on Market Hill, and spent his remaining years in Woodbridge. He died on 14th June, 1883, and was buried in a plain earthen grave beside the family vault in Boulge church.

In 1884 a journalist, William Simpson, travelled through Naishapur and collected seeds from the roses growing on Omar Khayyam's grave. These were germinated at Kew Gardens and in 1893 the Omar Khayyam club planted them on Fitzgerald's grave at Boulge. In February 1972 a member of the Persian Embassy repeated the ceremony by planting another six roses on the poet's grave to mark the 2,500th anniversary of the Persian empire and to honour the man who made his country's poetry popular.

New Street was constructed five hundred years ago to facilitate access between Market Hill and the quay. The Tudor inn, the Bell and Steelyard, is half way down and still has the weighing apparatus, a graduated arm with a sliding weight, which was used between the seventeenth and nineteenth centuries to weigh loaded carts, suspending them with straps from one end and then counterpoising by moving a lead weight along the notched beam.

Men have been building ships and messing about in boats in Woodbridge since Tudor times and before that. The greatest activity was in the seventeenth century when merchant ships and Men-of-War were built for the Navy.

From the quay I took a ferry boat (provided by the Sutton Hoo Society and running occasionally in the summer months) across the river and walked up the slope to the Anglo-Saxon burial site at Sutton Hoo. The alternative route to reach Sutton Hoo is to continue along the footpath upstream beside the river and then cross Wilford Bridge, taking the road towards Bawdsey ferry, on which there is a public footpath at the first fork in the road, leading to the right across the fields to Sutton Hoo.

In the summer of 1939 the tallest of the fifteen or so barrows on the Sutton Hoo burial site was excavated, to reveal the imprint in the soft sand of a boat over eighty feet long, the largest of its time ever found. In the centre was a pagan burial chamber that yielded the richest treasure ever dug from British soil. The boat, which was propelled by thirty-eight oarsmen and had no evidence of any mast, had been built about AD 610. It was in a poor state of repair by the time it was man-handled half a mile up a hundred foot slope from the river and lowered into a trench, as a coffin is lowered into a grave. A twelve foot burial mound was built above it.

The burial chamber contained the regalia of a chieftain or king, an iron stand and an unused whetstone, and his armour, sword, shield and helmet in a style similar to those of the period found in Sweden. Silver bowls, dishes and spoons with Christian connotations were unearthed with gold jewellery, clasps, a buckle and the lid of a purse which contained thirty-seven gold coins, also three blanks and two ingots, each one originating from a different place in France. Numismatic evidence from these coins gives the accepted date of the burial between AD 615 and 640. Cooking utensils, cauldrons and buckets were also recovered but no positive identifiable trace of a body. Thus began the enigma of Sutton Hoo.

Historians who believe that the boat did not contain a body consider that it might be a cenotaph to an East Anglian king, while others believe that a body was buried in the boat but has been decomposed by the well-aerated acidic sandy soil. Most historians however believe that there was a body and that it was probably that of King Redwald, a bretwalda or over-king, the first of the East Anglian kings to be converted to Christianity.

In 1984 Martin Carver, with a team of archaeologists from Birmingham University, embarked on a site evaluation of Sutton Hoo as the first stage in the systematic scientific exploration of the Sutton Hoo site. The team started in the surrounding fields, where they collected over five thousand pieces of pre-historic pottery and flint, and also uncovered the remains of a pre-historic hearth. A mobile radar unit crawled over the burial mounds hoping to detect their contents without the need for excavations, and a few promising shadows have shown up. Metal detectors found shells and bullets left from the Second World War, as the site was used as a battle training ground.

Delicate excavations twelve inches below the plough soil beyond the eastern edge of the present site exposed the remains or, more accurately, soil stains, of Anglo-Saxons buried in shallow flat graves. As the bodies decomposed they coloured the soil a darker brown than the surrounding sand, and remaining bone fragments glowed in the presence of ultra-violet light. Careful trowelling isolates the darker soil, revealing the form of the "sandmen". Exacting trowelling is required to unearth the sandman—each one requiring several days to isolate. In contrast the original 1939 excavation had taken only ten days to completely empty the boat grave of its contents; it would not be surprising that if sand traces of an Anglo-Saxon had been within the grave, they could have been missed. The sandmen lay in various directions, some on top of others, indicating that pagan and Christian burials took place here over various periods of time.

Trowelling has also unearthed Neolithic coarse-ware pots, Bronze Age ditches and a series of palisade ditches of unknown date. It is now realized that the burial site is twice the size it was first thought to be and that men had settled here as Neolithic farmers, followed by the Beaker people and then by Iron Age man, before the Anglo-Saxons took it over. Perhaps they will find here Rendil's steading, or royal residence, first mentioned by the historian Bede in the seventh century as being at Rendlesham four miles away:

> Swidhelm who had been baptised by Cedd in the province of the East Angles at the king's country seat of Rendlesham, that is Rendil's Steading or house.

If so, it will probably be similar in style to the palace of the Northumbrian king Edwin, which was discovered at Yeavering close to an Anglo-Saxon fort.

If the boat grave of a thousand and more years ago is an enigma, no less a mystery is the reported landing of a flying saucer in Rendlesham Forest a couple of miles to the east of Sutton Hoo. At the end of December, 1980, numerous sightings of mysterious lights in the sky above Woodbridge were seen and a particularly bright light reported by a local farmer which hovered for twenty minutes or more above the forest on 30th December. Aircraft were constantly taking off and landing from RAF Woodbridge and Bentwaters, but that same night a Norfolk civilian radar station logged the tracking of a UFO proceeding south towards Woodbridge. Early in January, 1981, the British UFO Research Association is reported to have been contacted by a high-ranking officer from Woodbridge air base, who told them that a UFO had come down in the forest and that he and the base commander had talked to small aliens three feet tall, suspended in shafts of light outside their craft.

These stories were widely circulated in the vicinity and published in the local paper. Surely Redwald, who departed this life in a phantom rowing boat, could not have returned fourteen hundred years later in a flying saucer! Perhaps Redwald's ghost lingers on at Rendlesham Church, where Bede said he had a palace and where his crown of gold was found in 1690.

From the ferry I climbed the steps cut into the soft, sandy cliff face and followed the edge of the trees, always keeping them on my left, until I came to a metalled road which leads to Haddon Hall. I turned right on to it for a hundred yards and then took the path to the left across the fields to Methersgate Hall. The footpath, in an anti-clockwise direction, is well marked round the Hall and passes to the front of this rambling residence with extensive lawns defended by old cannons. Just beyond this point the path follows the edge of a field down to the river (Methersgate quay is private property and has no right of way), from where I walked to Stonner Point opposite Waldringfield. Here a footpath returns to the largely private estate of Sutton village and Sutton Hall, the home of Sir Anthony Quilter, the descendant of Sir Cuthbert of Bawdsey Manor, and where Roman coins and a Roman urn have been found.

Mary Sewell, the first English writer to have a million copies of her work sold, was born at Sutton. Her daughter, Anna, is best known for her solitary literary work—*Black Beauty*.

The neighbouring village of Shottisham, just off the main Bawdsey road, is solitary, peaceful, unspoilt and picturesque. It is one of several places in Suffolk where King Edmund is said to have been martyred. Its pillory on the village green in front of the five-hundred-year-old pink-washed thatched pub, The Sorrel Horse, is not quite as old as you would imagine.

From Stonner Point it is a short, gentle stroll along the sea wall to the Ramsholt Arms, but it is a hard walk through the country lanes to reach the beginning of the Heritage Coast at Alderton, from where thirty-five miles of almost continuous footpaths complete the walk to Lowestoft, without touching the road.

Gathering the harvest at Holbrook.

# CHAPTER THREE

# The Heritage Coast Walk— Alderton to Aldeburgh

AT Alderton the coastal path starts behind the grocer's shop at the apex of a sharp bend in the road and conveniently, for the return walk, nearly opposite the Swan Inn. This is the point at which those walking from Bawdsey Ferry join the path, having scrambled over the shingle and having walked past the massive concrete gun emplacements on Bawdsey shore left over from the Second World War, edifices which with the Martello towers are permanent landmarks in our island history. The beaches here are littered with remnants of coastal defences, concrete blocks and barbed wire, and these probably still protect some of the rare plants struggling for existence.

I came to Shingle Street, which has been designated a Site of Special Scientific Interest, its beginning marked by Martello tower (AA). It is three kilometres long and has the third largest pure shingle deposit in Britain. The mouth of the river Ore at the north end of the beach separates it from Orford beach and the eight kilometres of shingle spit is formed by the North Sea meeting the coastline at an oblique angle, pushing the shingle and silt in a southerly direction until it comes to the mouth of the river, where it is slowed by contrary currents and deposited.

By the twelfth century the spit had reached Orford and was south of Butley Creek by the seventeenth century. It has been estimated that over the centuries the spit has grown at a rate of fourteen yards a year, but recently it has accelerated to fifteen yards. Shingle beaches border about a quarter of Britain's coastline, most of them devoid of vegetation, but a few sites—particularly the Suffolk shingle—can support plants which have adapted themselves to a moving hostile environment. On Orfordness and south of the tower at Shingle Street, yellow horned poppies are prominent, as is sea kale and occasionally herb robert, normally a woodland plant, and the now rare sea pea which allegedly prevented the people of Orford dying of starvation during a famine in the Middle Ages. The survival of these plants depends on the existence of small amounts of soil and humus between the pebbles into which the plants can extend their long roots. On more stable shingle, where the humus has built up, grow sea campion, sea thrift and biting stonecrop.

**Opposite page:** Shingle Street.

Shingle Street was evacuated in 1940 and taken over by the Army as a battle training area. The RAF bombed it for practice! There is still military mystery surrounding Shingle Street which will not be revealed for a period of seventy-five years from the last war, although the normal period of secrecy under the Official Secrets Act is only thirty years.

One of several stories, including the testing of the first atomic bomb at Shingle Street, suggests that a fragmentation bomb was tested here. Perhaps the Services are just too embarrassed about destroying the village pub! A Wellington bomber, using the Martello tower as a practice target, missed it and demolished the Lifeboat Inn, famous before the war for its lobster teas.

During the last war the RAF released hydrogen-filled balloons that drifted over the North Sea to occupied Europe trailing piano wires, supposedly to short-circuit overhead cables. Some carried phosphorus bombs, which acted as incendiary devices on landing. It was a comical sight to see a parade of RAF personnel marching in single file to the beach each carrying a balloon!

From the Coastguard cottages the path goes inland for about half a mile along the road to Hollesley. On the right hand side is a six-foot chain-link fence but fortunately there is also an eight-foot stile over which to continue along the sea wall in front of the Hollesley Bay Colony, now Her Majesty's Youth Custody and Detention Centre.

The detention centre takes its name from the Colonial College and Training Farm established in 1886 by Professor Robert Johnson under the auspices of the Agents General of the Colonies, and other distinguished persons, to train unqualified young gentlemen of means who wished to settle and make their careers in the British Colonies. Frequently such young men going abroad for the first time were ignorant of the conditions they would meet, the value of land or its proper management and were easily duped and lost their money. The college first set out to assess the aptitude of its students for a pioneering life and acquainted them with the hardships, including the hostile climates they would encounter abroad. They were trained to be self reliant, resourceful and self respecting. The curriculum included farming, animal husbandry, forestry, fruit growing, mineralogy, surveying, levelling, building, ploughing, smithing, carpentry, gardening, metallurgy, prospecting and chemistry. Through its contacts, particularly its former students abroad, the college became a colonial information centre. Unfortunately it ran into financial difficulties. From 1906 it was used as a training centre for the unemployed until it became part of the prison estate in 1939. It is now the largest penal holding in the prison service and occupies something like sixteen hundred acres, which also supports a herd of milking cows, pigs, a small flock of ewes and the famous Suffolk Punch horses.

This fine breed of horse, the pride of the county, is indigenous to this strip of the Suffolk coast, known as the Sandlings after the type of soil found here. During the early eighteenth century there were five families of Suffolk horse:

Blake, Attleborough, Shadingfield, Samsons and the famous Thomas Crisp's horse of Ufford, foaled two centuries ago, whose progeny succeeded in establishing themselves over the others. Every Suffolk Punch now alive can trace its pedigree back in the male line to the Ufford horse.

In 1771 Arthur Young, an agricultural writer, wrote of the Suffolk Punch:

> The breed of horses peculiar to this county is one of the great curiosities in it. I never yet saw any that are comparable to them in shape or the amazing power they have in drawing. They are called the Sorrel breed, the colour a bay sorrel. The form, that of a true round barrel, remarkably short, and the legs the same, and lower over the forehead than in any part of the back.

The Hollesley Bay stud was established during the middle of the nineteenth century by John Barthorp on the Red House estates which he farmed at Hollesley and which became the property of the Colonial College. In 1938 when the stud was acquired by the Prison Commissioners there were seventy-two Suffolk Punches with twenty-three foals born that year. The stud is now maintained at about thirty-six horses, which are used for ploughing, harrowing, and hauling and, appropriately, some have followed the Pilgrim Fathers to America to start a colony there.

Flybury Point is on the edge of Boyton Marshes at the mouth of the Butley River. As I sat and idly watched the cattle grazing from the vantage point of an old farm gate, I became conscious of my own isolation in this, the wildest and remotest part of Suffolk, accessible only on foot or by boat. There was bird life in profusion, and as I watched it through my binoculars a very large notice board came into focus with Havergate Island, RSPB Bird Sanctuary written on it. The magic was broken. Human beings had been here before me! I felt it to be an intrusion on my privacy, like finding a can of beans on an iceberg. The cattle wandered across the footpath on the sea wall ahead. Perhaps it was my isolated position that made me wonder if there was a bull amongst them!

Since the Wildlife and Countryside Act was passed in 1981, farmers have been permitted to put a bull in with cows and heifers on a field across which there is a public right of way. The law states:

> 59–(1) If, in a case not falling within subsection (2), the occupier of a field or enclosure crossed by a right of way to which this Part applies permits a bull to be at large in the field or enclosure, he shall be liable on summary conviction to a fine not exceeding £200.
>   (2) Subsection (1) shall not apply to any bull which—(a) does not exceed the age of ten months or
>     (b) is not of a recognised dairy breed and is at large in any field or enclosure in which cows or heifers are also at large.

A recognized dairy breed means Ayrshires, British Friesian, British Holstein, Dairy Shorthorn, Guernsey, Jersey and Kerry—breeds which are instantly recognized by the average walker! In short a beef breed of bull grazing

A couple of working pals at the Woodbridge Show.

Beware of the bull.

with cows is supposed to be safe. Don't believe it! I have discussed this subject with farmer friends and agricultural colleges, whose unanimous advice is: NEVER TRUST ANY BULL—particularly if you are accompanied by a dog or a child in a pushchair. "Beware of the Bull" signs take away the walker's rights, but better this than his life. If confronted by a bull, one farmer advised me to stand my ground, stare it out, wave my arms and shout and, with luck, the bull will take fright and back off. And what if it doesn't? The Ramblers' Association quote several horrific incidents with bulls and walkers. One young farmer had to rescue a walker outside Manchester by hitting the bull about the nose with a spade. Hopefully the Wildlife Act will be amended to afford protection to people as well as animals, but in the meantime BEWARE OF THE BULL!.

A fine specimen of cattle faced me and refused to give way; both sexes looked the same from this position and it was difficult to see what accoutrements it carried behind. However it hadn't a ring in its nose so I walked round the handsome beast and turned inland along the bank of the Butley river past an old jetty and then left the sea wall to climb up onto Burrow Hill. From this low historic mound, once an island surrounded by marshes, there are extensive views of the Suffolk countryside and of the Butley river.

It was on the summit of Burrow Hill that I was privileged to meet Valerie Fenwick, a remarkable lady and famous archaeologist. She is probably best known for her work during the 1965–69 excavation of the Sutton Hoo boat grave when she was the assistant to the Director, Bruce-Mitford. I had admired some of her work in the British Museum, in particular a huge cauldron suspended from the ceiling by ornate metal chains, which she had reconstructed from the corroded remains found in the boat grave. She was now digging for clues of past civilizations which once inhabited the hill. In 1983 they uncovered the remains of a small igloo-shaped kiln; Newcastle University gave it a date of AD 830. The team, with the help of a local potter, Eric Rowe, built an identical kiln alongside it and used it to fire pots as the villagers would have done during the middle of the Saxon period. In 1980 Valerie Fenwick had uncovered an inhumation cemetery on the hill, some of the bodies buried in coffins hewn out of one piece of wood, monoxylous, and found by radio-carbon dating to belong to a period around AD 780.

To the south of this cemetery a coin and a concentration of post holes gave a clue to at least two phases of occupation of the hill, the earlier habitation being dated to the late seventh century. The cemetery and settlements, which appear to have been enclosed by V-shaped ditches, were found to contain food debris, writing implements, window glass and evidence that these people were able to produce very fine textiles. This archaeological dig illustrates that after the departure of the Romans from East Anglia and before the Vikings devastated the area, people were living on Burrow Hill. These folk had trade contacts with Kent and northern France, were literate and enjoyed a high standard of living.

Valerie Fenwick (third from left) with archaeologists admiring the kiln of the Saxon period they had unearthed on Burrow Hill.

When gravel was taken from the top of the hill to make the local roads, about two hundred skeletons, mostly male, were uncovered. Valerie Fenwick told me that she found it quite astonishing that more than six hundred people were buried on the top of Burrow Hill. The local people have always known about the skeletons on the hill. Will Pettit, at ninety-six, remembered skulls in the gravel being carted from the hill sixty-five years before; so many were there that they were buried within the gravel beneath the road in Butley Street. A local legend associates the skeletons with a battle on the hill at which King Edmund, the last king of the East Angles, was defeated by the Vikings. He fled south to the village of Shottisham, where he was martyred. A variation of this story, recorded by an eleventh-century historian from Bury St Edmunds, who based his information on Suffolk tradition, states that the martyred king was first buried at Sutton (were his ancestors at Sutton Hoo?) near his royal residence, before being taken to his final resting place at Bury St Edmunds in the AD 930s.

I struck north along a farm track to Butley Corner, where I turned left and took the public footpath which led from the right hand side of the lane to Chillesford. Before doing so I continued along the lane and over the crossroads to visit the remains of Butley Priory, its ornate fourteenth-century gatehouse decorated with heraldic shields, some of which belonged to the English nobility and gentry who had been the Priory's benefactors. Pevsner described this gatehouse as, "One of the most ambitious and interesting buildings of the fourteenth century in Suffolk."

The heraldic shield in the middle of the bottom row is that of Ranulph de Glanvil who founded the Priory in 1171 as a House for Austin Canons. He was the Lord Chief Justice of Henry II and was also the founder of Leiston Abbey. The buildings at Butley occupied twenty acres surrounded by a stone wall. A single arch is now all that remains of the massive thirteenth-century church, 235 feet long, in which Michael de la Pole, Earl of Suffolk, was buried after he had been killed in the Battle of Agincourt. A local story says he was buried in a silver coffin, but it has never been found. Parts of the reredorter (toilets) and the

The Gatehouse of Butley Priory.

62

refectory are contained in the present buildings at Abbey Farm, which now occupy the site. The stone for the Priory buildings was brought by boat from the Yonne valley in France and landed at the Priory wharf, as then the sea came up to the Priory boundary. A medieval wharf was discovered in 1933.

The Priory was well endowed, and with an annual income of £318 from its estates was, after Bury St Edmunds, the richest in Suffolk. There was hardly a religious house in England that had so much patronage or such a wealth of appropriations. It is recorded as owning thirty-six churches, fourteen manors, the mill at Chillesford, two rabbit warrens and heaven alone knows how many rabbits. It also owned the manor at West Somerton in Norfolk, where there was a leper colony, but it is unlikely those unfortunate people fared well under the monks. Thomas, Duke of Norfolk, visited Butley in 1529 and sold the ancient forest, known as Staverton Park, to the Prior. It is about a mile north of the Priory and joined to it by a road, the Pilgrim's Way, along which are planted trees grouped in fives to symbolize the five wounds of Christ. The oldest part of the forest, known as The Thicks, through which the B 1084 passes from Butley to Bromeswell, contains oak trees up to four hundred years old descended from the primaeval forest which once covered eighty per cent of England.

A story relating to the forest recalls that a landowner in the distant past had several sons. Each would inherit land on the death of the elder brother, on condition that he cultivated it and reaped the harvest. One son, not liking his younger brother, sowed the fields with acorns. The crop has not yet been harvested! It is thought that the forest was spared the woodman's axe when it was turned into a deer park during the thirteenth century. Deer still roam in the forest, mainly roe and fallow, while there is now a red deer farm in the middle of the park, also noted for the height of its holly tree. Traffic noise does not seem to disturb the deer and I often stand on the roadside and watch them strolling until the snap of a twig underfoot sends them scurrying away. Whilst I was driving through late one night, my headlights lit up a doe with her fawn as they were crossing the road ahead. Sadly these deer become the victims of a number of road accidents.

1539 saw the dissolution of Butley Priory along with the other monastic establishments in England, as decreed by Henry VIII. The following year it was granted to the Duke of Norfolk, but then he sold it in 1544 to William Forth, a rich Hadleigh clothier. He must have been pleased to be able to buy himself into the land of the blessed. The old gatehouse was converted into a residence in 1737 and, for a time, served as the vicarage. One room in the gatehouse, the ghost room, was kept sealed. It has been suggested that it contained the ghost of Robert Brommer, a Prior in the reign of Henry VII, who had got into debt and committed suicide.

I returned to the footpath to continue my journey to Chillesford across the Sandlings. It is a miracle that anything can grow in this dry earth, but carrots like

Deer can frequently be seen crossing the roads around Butley.

it and have been grown here for generations. They were exported to London during the seventeenth century and were then used to nurture the famous horses of the Suffolk Sandlings, although rabbits and hares took their fair share. Arthur Young writing in 1813 commended the carrot as the best food for the cart horse but not the coach horse, who had to move faster. It was about this time that the Suffolk Punch was being bred into an elegant horse for drawing coaches in preference to the plough. Arthur Young wrote:

> Horses are never in such good condition as on carrots. If oats and carrots are given at the same time, they leave the oats and eat the carrots, but for horses that are rode fast they are not equally proper.

64

I stood on the first piece of metalled road since I left Shingle Street. To the left the narrow lane wended its way to Neutral Farm, where Saxon relics were discovered, thought to be of the same period as Sutton Hoo. Pieces of bronze and pottery have been turned up by the plough and further investigation exposed post holes, all that remained of Saxon huts, and a hearth, near which was found the remains of an ox's head with a spear embedded in it, dated about AD 500: there are indications that a row of Saxon huts once stood here. Further on, at a sharp corner, is the Butt and Oyster pub—the Butt here refers to a flat fish as in halibut. Beyond are the ancient Butley Woods, carpeted by daffodils in spring, when the public flock to see them.

The coastal path follows the lane in the opposite direction past the Butley Mills, situated at the head of the tidal estuary at Butley Creek.

Butley Mills has been in the Hewitt family for generations. John Hewitt acquired seven farms during the depression in the 1920s, as well as managing the mill. Both his grandparents died of smallpox when they were young leaving their daughter, Edith—his mother—to be brought up by a great aunt, who managed the mill herself until Tom Hewitt came from Norfolk as manager and married Edith. John was a clever boy who attended Woodbridge School and was being groomed for university; however, he decided to leave school at sixteen to work as a lorry driver earning ten shillings a week. This he paid to a man for looking after his pigs, which he reared and sold, and in this way began his business and farming career. When asked if he regretted not going to university he replied, "Good heavens no, I might have spent my life working for somebody else like, perhaps, Pauls the Ipswich millers."

Another visitor to Butley Mills in the 1950s was the world famous bird photographer, Eric Hosking. Eric was particularly fond of owls, although one was responsible for the loss of sight in one of his eyes. Many of his best owl photographs were taken across the creek at Chillesford Lodge, and in *The Times*, on 13th September, 1950, he recorded the return of the avocets to Havergate Island and Butley Creek.

John Hewitt began the custom of giving his daughter, Rachel, a family heirloom on her birthday, and kindled in her a passion for antiques and bygones. Rachel soon had many items: "They were literally falling off the walls of my home", she said. Her solution was to open the Chillesford Rural Relics Museum in the old stables at her home, Hill Farm. She displayed tools once used by the cobbler, cooper, miller, saddlemaker, the vet and the milkmaid.

Roger Chilvers, the local thatcher, exhibited his craft using Chillesford reed, considered the best, cut from the extensive reed beds at the head of Butley Creek opposite the mill.

I visited Glyn Evans, Rachel's neighbour, who also collects rural memorabilia. Here I was amused by a flush toilet which discharged sawdust and not water. Glyn demonstrated one of the earliest vacuum cleaners, operated by hand pump—but a dustpan and brush would have been less agony! There was an automatic mousetrap which tipped its unfortunate victim into a jam jar of water, then automatically reset itself ready for the next victim. Hung in a corner was the bottom half of a coffin, a reminder of the difficulty of carrying the deceased down the twisting narrow stairs of country cottages. The hokey-pokey, similar in shape to an egg cup, once had ice-cream served in it; the costrel, a small barrow or firkin, once contained liquid refreshment for the labourers in the fields, while the chrondometer was filled with grain to find its density.

From Butley Mills, the lane reaches the main Orford Road (B 1084) in the middle of Chillesford—chilles from chesil, meaning gravel, and so gravel ford, which is believed to have been near the church. The ancient church tower is made from local coralline crag. This was struck by lightning in 1874, fusing the bells into a shapeless spoil. Nearby the jawbone of a whale was dug out of an old brickyard. The whale got there, it is said, by swimming up the river, which at that time was a tributary of the river Rhine. The mass graves of those villagers who succumbed to the Plague have also been unearthed here.

The ancient Froize Inn, parts of which date back to the fifteenth century, is a few yards in the opposite direction towards Orford. A froize is a thick pancake often served with bacon and, according to the local paper, was served to hungry passing wayfarers in the 1730s by monks who owned the inn. The Froize has been referred to as Fry's Inn, the name of a local lane. This may be a derivation from friars or from frig, the ancient goddess of fertility after whom Friday is named, but the pancake has it hands down. Pancakes were not on the menu when I entered the pub, although they are on Shrove Tuesday, and I contented myself instead with a substantial ham sandwich, like those we called door stoppers when I was a boy; washed down with a pint of real ale.

The coastal path continues north almost opposite the Froize through Tunstall Forest to Iken village, but before walking it I took the path from the Orford side of the Froize Inn through Sudbourne Park to the ancient port and delightful village of Orford—a gem in the crown of Suffolk jewels.

Sudbourne Hall has been pulled down, but its outbuildings have been converted into flats and maisonettes. The tell-tale signs of former opulence remain: the outline of well laid-out gardens crossed by a carriageway, guarded by ornate iron gates and punctuated with giant stone flower vases standing on decorative pedestals. The cricket pitch with the typically English pavilion behind it is an idyllic setting, still used and a reminder of the great sporting tradition of this place, although the sport was not always cricket. In 1901 over thirty-five thousand game were bagged in one season, including hare, pheasant, partridge and rabbits. Behind the Froize Inn is the remains of a duck decoy; the bag would have contained widgeon, teal, pintail, pochard, water hen, knot, woodcock, snipe, jack snipe, golden plover and grey plover. Hardly my idea of sport. It is no wonder that so many species are now on the protected list.

An unusual cottage on the Sudbourne estate near Orford.

The original Hall was built in the early seventeenth century by Sir Michael Stanhope. He was attendant upon Queen Elizabeth I at her Privy Chamber, and his remains lie in Sudbourne Church beneath a richly decorated tomb on which kneels his effigy. The second Hall was built in the Palladian style by James Wyatt about 1784. It was a plain rectangular brick structure with a Neo-Classical exterior, situated in eleven thousand acres of the best shooting land in Suffolk. Avenues of chestnut, elm and beech trees radiated from the front door. Inside there were fifty rooms, thirty-six bedrooms—thirteen of which housed the seventy servants—eight bathrooms and six reception rooms. The pride of the house was its massive hall, with a very high ceiling and a staircase that had two hundred and fifty pillars on the balustrading, each with a different Italianate carving. The house was owned by Francis Seymour-Conway, the Third Marquess of Hertford, Earl of Yarmouth. On his twenty-first birthday in 1798 he became a Tory MP for the family borough of Orford. He was succeeded by his son the Fourth Marquess, who, although unmarried at eighteen became the father of Richard Wallace. It was Richard who laid out the extensive gardens at Sudbourne. Both the Third and Fourth Marquess were avid collectors of great works of art, paintings, French furniture, sculpture and tapestries and these were inherited by Richard Wallace, who eventually married a French woman, Julie Castelnau, the mother of his thirty-year-old son. When Richard Wallace died she carried out his wish that the greater part of the collection be left to the nation on condition that the Government provided suitable premises for it, and that no other works of art were to be added to the collection. The Government purchased the lease of Hertford House in Manchester Square, London (just behind Selfridges in Oxford Street), which belonged to the Hertford family. This museum housing the "Wallace Collection" was opened on 22nd June, 1900, by the Prince of Wales. The best-known painting is "The Laughing Cavalier" by Frans Hals, which hangs on the first floor, and the collection is described as one of the finest picture galleries in the world.

Sudbourne Hall was purchased in 1904 by Kenneth Mackenzie Clark, whose family fortunes came from the early nineteenth century textile industry when Patrick Clark developed a cotton heddle loop to replace the silk ones from Hamburg that became unobtainable during the Napoleonic wars. The thread was found to be suitable for sewing and was sold wound on to a cotton bobbin, also invented by the Clarks. They opened a factory in Paisley, Scotland, in 1813 with the slogan:

It's Paisley thread that holds the world together.

On 13th July, 1903, a year before they moved to Sudbourne, Kenneth Clark was born. He became widely known through his television series "Civilisation". The little boy spent his formative years at Sudbourne Hall, because the family came to their Suffolk home each autumn for the shooting. This lasted from September until the end of January, when the family moved to the French Riviera. Kenneth Clark Senior was an alcoholic but this did not deter his good gambling fortune and he became known as: "the man who broke the bank at Monte Carlo".

Young Kenneth was sent back to Sudbourne during the summer months in the charge of his nanny, while his parents continued to live it up abroad. He was badly treated by the servants, who gave him rotten food to eat; worm-eaten cheese, curdled milk, rancid butter and bitter fruit whilst they feasted off the best. He did however enjoy going to Aldeburgh in the governess cart, and there he would wander along the beach picking up pebbles and looking for amber; if he failed, he would go along to Mr Stephenson's amber shop and purchase a piece on his way home. In later years he returned to Aldeburgh, usually staying at the Wentworth or with Mary Potter the wife of the humorist Stephen Potter. He said the atmosphere there cleared his mind and sharpened his focus when he had a difficult piece of writing to complete. He would stroll along the shore searching for words and ideas as once he had searched for amber and pebbles. The beauty of the Suffolk coast became the standard by which Kenneth Clark judged all other landscapes.

When he was eight years old he was sent to prep school, now called Ludgrove, at Wokingham, after which he completed his education with five years at Winchester before becoming a student at Trinity College, Oxford. As Director of the National Gallery, Chairman of the Arts Council and Surveyor of the King's Pictures, he influenced the work of many of the great British artists including Graham Sutherland and the sculptor Henry Moore. He was awarded a KCB in 1938, a Life Peerage in 1969 and the Order of Merit. When he was Chancellor of York University, I was privileged to have the degree of Bachelor of Philosophy conferred on me by him.

The village pump at Orford.

Orford Castle (of which only the keep remains) was built by Henry II, best known for his involvement in the murder of Thomas Becket, Archbishop of Canterbury, and for the foundation of the present jury system. He came to the throne in AD 1154 after a period of anarchy when powerful barons held sway.

The steps of Orford Castle.

In Suffolk, Hugh Bigod—Earl of Norfolk—was the most powerful and he had castles at Walton (now under the sea off Felixstowe), Framlingham, Bungay and Thetford. In 1157 Henry confiscated these castles but gave Framlingham and Bungay back in 1165 on payment of a fine. In the same year building commenced on Henry's royal castle at Orford, which was completed in 1173. This was the year of rebellion against the King led by his eldest son, also Henry. An army of Flemish mercenaries, under the Earl of Leicester, first attacked Dunwich but were repulsed and then attacked Walton Castle, which by now must have been in the hands of the King again, before they went on to attack the castle at Framlingham. No doubt Orford Castle exerted its influence, but it doesn't seem to have been attacked, although minor repairs were done to it at the end of the rebellion. The rebels lost and the castles of Walton and Framlingham were destroyed.

In 1215 King John was in East Anglia busily suppressing the barons and captured Framlingham from Roger Bigod. After his death the barons appealed to the French King's son, Prince Louis, who was offered the English crown. The prince invaded and many castles, including Orford, were surrendered to him, although not enough to win him the crown, which was taken by the young King, Henry III. Orford Castle was finally taken out of military service in the fourteenth century when it was granted to Robert Ufford in 1336. He was created Earl of Suffolk in the following year. It remained in civilian hands until it was bought by Sir Arthur Churchman, was presented to the Orford Town Trust in 1930 and passed into the custody of the state under the Ancient Monuments Act of 1962. The keep, which was once surrounded by a bailey and a castle wall interspersed with rectangular towers, is now all that remains of the original castle. It is ninety feet high and has a basement, lower and upper halls and a roof level with turrets, and can be seen twenty-five miles out to sea. This probably prevented it from being pulled down, as it was an indispensable landmark. It was constructed mainly with local stone—septaria, obtained from the estuary mud—and with stone brought from Caen in Normandy, which was used to make the various angles and the plinth on which it now stands. The keep was constructed in a revolutionary polygonal shape, which superseded the original Norman square or rectangular shape. It is now in excellent condition and very impressive, a child's idea of a real castle.

No doubt the castle dungeons held their fair share of prisoners, who would have endured a barbarous torture associated with the period, but only one is recorded—the "Orford Merman". He was caught up in fishermen's nets and brought to the castle. The chronicler, Ralph of Coggeshall, monk, recorded the event, which he said took place about the time as the castle was being built. He described the man as being naked and hairy with a long beard and "being as a man in all his members", but there was no mention of a tail. He had a good appetite, was not religious and did not speak, although to encourage him they hung him up by his feet and tortured him. Happily the unfortunate man, not having enjoyed his taste of civilization, managed to escape back to the sea. The merman's tale (or tail?) is perpetuated in the sign of the famous fish restaurant the Butley-Orford Oysterage, now one of Orford's main attractions, originally owned and run by the late Richard Pinney.

I first met Richard Pinney at his home set within the shadow of the castle. He was one of those rare talented characters who could successfully turn his hand to anything. Resourceful, tenacious, intuitive, industrious to a high degree, he emanated a quiet confidence and supreme optimism, and had a real love of the Suffolk countryside. In 1946 he gave up a good position in the City to live in the country. He chose Suffolk and leased a derelict cottage about a mile south of Orford on the bank of Butley Creek, almost opposite Burrow Hill. After restoring the Ferry Cottage, he turned his attention to making a living from the countryside. Wild rabbits were plentiful, but myxomatosis soon ended that. Richard Pinney founded the Deben Rush Weavers at Debenham, where baskets and mats were made. Harvesting rushes, which clogged the local rivers, was an arduous and uncomfortable job entailing standing waist deep in water whilst cutting the reeds on the river bed with a sickle. Locally cut rushes were insufficient, so they were harvested in other parts of the country and then imported from Holland, France and Portugal.

Richard Pinney then turned his attention to the sea and used his boat, *Ann*,

Billy Pinney at his smoke house down by the Butley River.

to fish in Hollesley Bay. He caught large sea trout close in to the shore and decided to try smoking them. He invented his own smoke box and burnt oak logs instead of the customary sawdust, and soon he was curing all kinds of fish.

Cultivating oysters in Butley Creek was an ambition he had nurtured since eating fried oysters and home-cured bacon at Orford's Crown and Castle Inn. He was encouraged by *Glimpses of a Norwich Expedition 1634–35*, in which it said:

> From Aldeburgh hasted I by Butley Abbey at which sweet sea, the fat and lazy abbots and the Monasticke Monks, in those their flourishing days, did take pleasure and delight, to cram and stuff their paunches with those solacious oysters on their fish eating days . . .

English oysters are seasonal, so Richard Pinney introduced a Portuguese variety into the once neglected beds of the Butley River, followed by a Japanese variety, *Gigas*, a strain better able to tolerate the low temperature of English winters. He then decided to open the fish restaurant, the Butley-Orford Oysterage, in Orford's market square. It was an immediate success. An article in the *Daily Telegraph* put the Oysterage into the gourmet guides and laid the foundation for the postal distribution of Pinney's smoked fish.

Richard's son, Billy, now lives at Ferry Cottage with his family. He does the smoking and looks after the oysters. For fishing he relies on fast motor boats to reach the Hollesley Bay fishing grounds and brings in catches including sole, plaice, skate, cod, lobsters and crabs for both the restaurant and the Lowestoft market. The enterprising Richard Pinney gained much from the remote muddy rivers and his story is told in his autobiography, *Smoked Salmon and Oysters*. Orford misses this sincere man, who died recently.

Across the square, just beyond the King's Head in Front Street, is the Orford Craft Shop, situated in mellow red brick outbuildings in which are displayed a vast variety of crafts and wicker baskets. The shop is owned by Stuart Bacon, underwater explorer extraordinary, who, with a team of divers, has been investigating the Suffolk seabed with a particular interest in the drowned ancient city of Dunwich. Stuart Bacon was born at Aldeburgh and as a child spent many happy hours discovering his native coastline. The stories of Dunwich fascinated him and since he became a qualified diver in 1971 he has led and organized regular underwater explorations. His team have located the ruins of four churches and brought ashore several artefacts from them. They can be seen in the Dunwich Museum and in his own Suffolk Underwater Studies Exhibition at the craft shop.

Exploration of the seabed is difficult, dark and dangerous. The divers prod the soft silt for artefacts with long metal rods known as excavators, which sound out objects. These are then lifted to the surface. Stuart and Jean Bacon are both historical writers and their books about the villages along the Suffolk coast are well known.

St Bartholomew's Church stands on the opposite side of the square to the

The Orford Craft Shop, run by the underwater sea diver Stuart Bacon.

castle and was once at the head of a tidal inlet into which ships sailed and tied up at the quay (on what is now Quay Street). The old church was begun in 1166, about the same time as the castle, and the ruins of the Norman chancel still stand outside the east end of the church, while some of it is incorporated into the present fourteenth-century building.

Under a carpet in the vestry on the north-east side of the church is a commemorative brass plate to John Coggeshall, three times Mayor of Orford, who was buried here on 23rd February, 1631, and according to the brass left five sons, two daughters and a virtuous wife. One son, Henry Coggeshall, 1623–90, portrayed on another brass, was an inventor, mathematician and author and is best known for the development of a slide rule used for calculating and costing the quantity of tree timber. His invention was described in his 1677 pamphlet:

Timber Measured by a Line of more Ease, Dispatch and Exactness than any other way now in use, by a Double Scale . . .

There is an example of the Coggeshall Slide Rule in the Science Museum and it was well used until the end of the nineteenth century.

74

Orford was an important medieval port, through which wool was exported and wine imported, and during the reign of Edward III it provided ships for his naval battles against France, notably at Sluys and the siege of Calais. Many ships came to grief on the Orfordness shingle. After a violent storm when thirty-two ships were wrecked, John Meldrum was granted the right to erect temporary lighthouses on Orfordness in 1634. He immediately sold this right to Alderman Gerard Gore, who built a high and a low lighthouse which ships aligned to steer between the shoals. They were described by Trinity House as being "very crazy". One of the first lighthouse keepers Gerard Gore employed was Mrs Bradshaw, continuing the work after the death of her husband. Unfortunately he had to dismiss her for inefficiency, but wrote:

According to my promise you have enjoyed the Light now till Christmas and I have had more complaints in this half year than ever I had in your father or husband's time. I did not think you would have been so careless but I excuse it because you are a woman. My will is that you deliver the House and Light and all things as such belong to the House and Light to the attention of the Bailiffs of the Town of Aldeburgh, so not doubting of your performance therein, I rest

Yours

Gerard Gore 1648

Havergate Island is a sanctuary of the Royal Society for the Protection of Birds. It lies in the middle of the river Ore with the mainland on one side and protected from the sea on the other side by Orfordness. According to Richard Cobbold, the sole occupant of the island in the eighteenth century was a shepherd who lived in the solitary red cottage and made smugglers welcome. It was here that the villainous smuggler John Luff died of his gunshot wounds after fighting with the coastguards, and Margaret Catchpole is supposed to have signalled to smugglers out at sea from an upstairs window. Before the Second World War the island was occupied by the Brinkley family, who grazed sheep and cattle brought over by ferry. During the war the island was used for target practice, and when a shell destroyed one of the sluices it flooded the southern part of the island turning it into a number of lagoons with protruding islands, an ideal spot for avocets. These birds bred regularly along the east coast until the nineteenth century, when egg and skin collectors reduced their numbers and drove them away. In 1947 four pairs returned to Havergate Island and four more to Minsmere. The next year the RSPB bought the island and it now has the largest colony of avocets in Britain.

Reg Partridge became the island's first RSPB warden in 1947. He was a professional yachtsman, sailing eight-metre yachts in the summer and fishing off Aldeburgh in the winter. He built sluices to control the water level and added to the lagoons and nesting sites for the avocets. In 1953 he was awarded the BEM for rescuing two policemen from drowning during the disastrous east coast floods and was also awarded the RSPB's Bronze award for his services to the birds. After his untimely death in 1974, his son John became the warden.

75

Avocets are not the only birds on the island, and on one occasion we admired a spoonbill which had just taken up occupancy of a lagoon island: the avocets then received about as much attention as the local sparrows! The return boat trip up the Narrows back to Orford is idyllic especially on a warm summer evening with the sun setting, the tide on the rise easing gently up the channel, the wind still and the water calm—time suspended. Waders including curlew quietly line the shore picking and pecking away at the mud.

From Orford I returned to Chillesford Froize Inn and picked up the coastal path almost opposite the Inn. I turned right at the cottages and followed the path across a meadow, where I met more cattle. However, as they were all lying down, it was difficult to detect the presence of a bull! They idly chewed cud and gave me a curious glance but I crossed without incident and entered Tunstall Forest, crossed over the B 1078 to Tunstall and immediately re-entered the forest on the other side of the road to emerge on the country road between Snape Maltings and Sudbourne. The path continues on the opposite side of the road, leading to Iken village and church at the Anchorage, overlooking the beautiful Alde estuary.

When I first came upon Iken Church in 1968, tragedy had just struck. Sparks from a bonfire had set the thatched roof alight and all that remained was a burnt-out shell. A makeshift chapel had been made in the chancel, which contains the shaft of an Anglo-Saxon cross discovered there. Church histories say there is nothing of note at Iken, but as I walked through the ruins and noted the displays of flowers lovingly placed amongst the ruins, and small items such as cards, notepaper and envelopes for sale, hoping to make a little money with which to pay for the restoration of their beautiful church, it made me think of hope and faith. The church has now been completely restored. The spirit of St Botolph, who built his monastery on this site thirteen hundred years ago, emanated from the crumbling walls. These ruins, overlooking the mudflats, blending with the winding river and open sky, added mystery to this beautiful place. Here is nothing. Here there is everything.

Botulf or Botolph was probably born a Saxon in East Anglia in AD 620. Having trained as a Benedictine monk at a monastery in north-east France, Formoutière-en-Brie, he became a chaplain in a nunnery. He requested from the King, probably King Anna or his brothers, Kings Ethelhere or Ethelwald, who succeeded him, a piece of land on which to build a monastery. He was given Icanhoe, "a dismal spot which was just a God forsaken devil possessed place surrounded by swamps". Icanhoe is generally agreed to be Iken, hoe meaning headland. Little else is recorded of Botolph's life, although it seems he was well liked and respected. He was visited by the noble Northumbrian, Ceolfrith, who took Botolph's ideas back to his part of the country. Botolph died and was buried at Icanhoe in 680. In 870 the Danes burnt his monastery and in 963 Ethelwold, the Bishop of Winchester, transferred Botolph's remains to Grundisburgh in

Iken church from the river.

Suffolk, where they remained in a chapel dedicated to him. Later the saint's body was divided between three caskets; the one containing his head went to Ely Cathedral, one went to Thorny Abbey and the third went to Bury St Edmunds and later to Westminster Abbey. Legend states that when St Botolph's remains were removed from Grundisburgh the night was pitch dark, but a column of light appeared behind the shrine in the chapel to help the priests. It is also believed that a golden calf, which once stood in St Botolph's chapel, still remains in the field where the chapel stood. In the Middle Ages, St Botolph was the saint associated with travellers—Botulf means boat help—and churches dedicated to the saint were often found at the entrance gates to walled towns. In a previous era the Romans had a settlement on a hill overlooking Iken and here Queen Boudicea with her Iceni tribes fought against them.

I retraced my steps at the Anchorage, where barges hove to awaiting a berth at Snape. Just after a sharp right-hand turn I found a footpath that took me down to the water's edge, along beside the river and through the reed beds to the old Maltings at Snape. This scenic walk with wide panoramic views across the estuary must be the most beautiful along the Suffolk coast. Half way along it at Iken Cliff there is a pleasant picnic site and unobtrusive car park, but no cliffs.

The Maltings are a unique collection of excellent Victorian industrial buildings which have now been converted into a concert hall, art gallery, wholefood and craft shops, a garden centre, restaurant, and a teashop. Country courses, excursions and walks are organized from here. It is an ideal place from which to start an exploration of the Suffolk coast.

The Maltings were constructed by Newson Garrett, the grandson of Richard Garrett, founder of the engineering works at Leiston. Newson, realizing that the business would pass eventually to his elder brother, decided to seek his fortune in London and became a pawnbroker in Whitechapel. There he married Louisa Dunnell, and had the first four of his ten children. They were to become a remarkable family. Elizabeth, against almost impossible opposition, became the first woman in England to qualify as a doctor and with her husband James Skelton Anderson founded a hospital in London which was entirely for women. She also became the first woman Mayor in England when she became Mayor of Aldeburgh in 1908. Her sister Millicent married Henry Fawcett, the blind Postmaster General, and became involved in the Suffragette movement; she was president of the National Union for Women's Suffrage Societies.

In 1841, when Newson was twenty-nine, he returned to Suffolk with his family to take over the business of Osborne and Fennel, corn and coal merchants, who operated from Snape quay. Snape lies only five miles from the sea, but the sailing distance is over twenty miles down the Alde and the Ore. It has been a port since Roman times. It was a rendezvous for the spritsail barges which brought in coal and took out grain for the breweries at Norwich and London. Barges still sail into Snape and tie up at the quay but now carry passengers on sight-seeing jaunts. Barges were also built and repaired here by Newson Garrett in a small dock situated on what is now the concert hall lawn. With the rapid expansion of his business Newson decided that instead of exporting barley to be made into malt by the brewer, he would make the malt himself at Snape and hence increase his profit. He commenced the building of the first of his four Maltings in 1846 with bricks from his own brickyard. In 1859 the Great Eastern Railway completed a mile and half track to join the Maltings to their main line at Saxmundham. Unfortunately the line terminated on the opposite side of the road and Suffolk Punches pulled wagons to and from the train.

Bob Ling was a maltster (as were his father and grandfather) before becoming the manager of the Snape Maltings concert hall. His father was the foreman of the last malthouse at Snape, built facing the river in 1900. The old barley store now houses the Peter Pears School of Music, the four kilns have become the concert hall, and the screening loft, where the dried culm from the kiln was separated from the malt, is a restaurant. The old malt store has been converted into changing rooms and the Bays, connecting the barley store with the kiln where the barley was germinated and where Bob Ling started work shovelling steeped barley onto the upper floor, is now the concert hall manager's flat. It was originally intended for Benjamin Britten.

**Opposite:** Jumbo's Cottage at Iken with the Heritage Coast Way crossing in front of it.

The former home of Benjamin Britten at Snape.

I sat with Bob Ling in his spacious, picturesque lounge and he told me about his life at the Maltings. He was born in Blaxhall in 1923; seven years later his family moved to Snape and Bob received a very practical kind of education under his headmaster Stanley Reeve. He learned to build chicken huts, gymnastic apparatus and bathing huts down by the river at Snape Bridge, where all the school children learned to swim.

"There was no vandalism then", said Bob. "After all you don't smash up what you have made yourself."

The children kept chickens, bought and sold eggs and learned their arithmetic by keeping the books. Any profits went towards equipment for the school. Bob worked on a poultry farm for two years, then at sixteen joined the day gang at the Maltings. They loaded railway trucks with twelve-stone sacks of finished malt, carried lengthwise across their shoulders and they then unloaded Welsh smokeless coal and coke for the furnaces. The gangers soon developed

Snape Maltings.

the knack of carrying the heavy sacks so that they could run with them along planks and into the wagons. However at the end of the each day, Bob said, "I could have jumped over the moon with the weight off my shoulders!" Working extra hard or tackling a dirty job could earn Hubble Money—threepence extra pay for unloading a truck of coal—and sometimes they would be rewarded with a brass beer token to exchange in the pub.

Only the best barley is used in malting. Originally this was grown locally, but with increasing demand it was imported from the Pacific coast, the Danube, Asia Minor, Tunis or Algeria and brought by barge from Calais. The grain was fed through chutes from the barley store into vast vats of water, called steeps, at the beginning of the Bays, where it was steeped for two or three days before being drained and spread out to germinate on the long floors. Bob remembers throwing the wet grain up on to the first floor as being particularly tough work.

If you didn't throw it far enough, it would run back down on top of you.

The temperature of the germinating barley was controlled by spreading it out on to the floors and then gradually working it along the floor until it reached the kiln after about eight days. By this time the barley had grown a shoot, or culm, and chemical processes had converted the starch in the barley grain to malt. This was later fermented into beer by the brewer. An elevator took the wet barley to a floor suspended above the kiln surface, on which it was spread and dried until it reached the correct colour for a particular beer. Stout required the malt to be heated longer to produce the darker colour and different flavour. The maltsters, including Bob, worked on the floor stripped to the waist wearing canvas rope-soled boots, not to protect their feet from the boiling heat, but to protect the malt from excessive crushing as they walked over it, turning it with their shovels! As the drying process began, the steam rising from the malt produced such a thick fog that the maltsters could not see beyond an arm's length. When it was over the sweet and brown malt was shovelled into the screening loft and shaken and sieved to remove the culm, which was used for animal feed, before being stored ready for the brewer.

Crystal malt, a variety used to make Ovaltine and Guinness, was also made at Snape. The longer-rooted barley was dried in cylinders rotating over the furnaces instead of being spread out on floors. If a grain of this malt was split open between the fingers, the interior resembled grains or crystals of brown sugar. Bob Ling worked in the engine room for sometime before the Maltings finally closed down in 1965. Work commenced at five in the morning and finished at three in the afternoon. The firemen, who lived on site, had longer shifts and were required to keep the furnaces well tended.

"Everything, including the gossip, started at the Maltings," said Bob, "The main talking point was the Works football team."

Most came to work by cycle and, as Bob said, "It was an unforgettable sight to watch a hundred employees cycling over Snape Bridge at lunch time."

Bob and Doris got about on bikes and, when their children were small, they rode in a go-cart fastened behind Bob's bike! When the Maltings closed, Bob and Doris took up contract grave digging to earn a living. Doris had the distinction of being the only Suffolk female in the trade. However, being small, she only dug the first four feet otherwise she could not have got out! In 1970 the couple had the opportunity to return to the Maltings when Bob became the concert hall manager, a position where he could exercise those practical and organizational skills picked up over the years. Bob and Doris have now retired. I hope Doris has fulfilled her ambition to spend time wandering idly through the rides of Tunstall Forest and then stopping at one of the local hostelries for lunch. Bob reckoned she would soon become bored but I doubt it, particularly as it comes close to my idea of heaven.

Newson Garrett died in 1893 and was buried in the family vault in Aldeburgh churchyard. His youngest son, George, continued to manage the

Maltings, which were taken over by S. Swonnell and Sons of Oulton Broad after the First World War. Modernization had brought an end to the traditional way of malting and the firm went into voluntary liquidation in 1964. The railway, which for some time had only been used to bring coal to the Maltings, had already succumbed to competition from road transport, and had closed in 1960. Thus ended 120 years of continuous malting at Snape. The buildings were not idle for long.

The Aldeburgh Festival, founded by Benjamin Britten, Peter Pears and Eric Crozier, was looking for a permanent concert hall for their annual event, which was attracting increasing audiences, and in 1966 they converted the largest malthouse, nearest the river, into a concert hall, which was opened by the Queen in 1967. Two years later it caught fire and was completely destroyed but was rebuilt and opened again in 1970. The Queen also attended the second opening. Snape Maltings has a world-wide reputation for its classical music performances and is unique in that it is situated in the heart of the countryside beside a peaceful river, which has inspired much of the music played there.

From the Maltings my journey took me over the Snape Bridge, at the head of the Alde estuary, and I turned right at the Crown a few yards up the road to make another delightful walk along the Sailor's Path; this was the route walked by sailors joining their ships at Aldeburgh. Snape is well endowed with good hostelries. The Plough and Sail at the Maltings is named after customers of days gone by who ploughed and harvested and then carried their crops in their own barges. The Crown had a reputation for harbouring smugglers: they were hidden in a windowless room with a trap door. A former landlord, Ted Pryke, introduced the growing of sugar beet into the area in 1911 and brought over some Dutch workers to help him. The Crown serves some interesting dishes, as does the Golden Key, round the corner.

Where the Sailor's Path meets the road at Snape a country lane leads north past Rookery Farm to a tumulus, or sepulchral mound, the sole survivor of six tumuli next to the main Aldeburgh road. This is the site of a British burial chamber, where burial urns have been found. In 1862 excavation of one of the tumuli exposed the outline of an Anglo-Saxon ship of the same period as Sutton Hoo. Again the rusted iron nails which held the ship's timbers together had remained in position marking the outline of the ship. It was about fifty feet long and ten feet wide at the beam, and dated between AD 635 and AD 650. Unlike the ship at Sutton Hoo it contained the skeletal remains of a body with a sword and blade lying alongside it. On a finger bone was a gold ring with an engraved stone worked by a Roman. The burial chamber also contained the fragments of a green vase and some auburn hair. Accounts vary as to the identity of the body occupying the boat. A Viking marauder has been suggested, and a wealthy local chieftain. Considerable archaeological excavation is now being undertaken at this site, which crosses the main Aldeburgh road.

The Sailor's Path comes out on the main Aldeburgh road (A 1094) about half a mile from the Aldeburgh Golf Club. It is a miserable walk along the main road into the town. However a footpath continues just beyond the Golf Club, where a cinder track meets the golf course at the Red House, the former home of Peter Pears and Benjamin Britten, and then joins the B 1122 to Leiston. Turn left and proceed down Warren Hill Lane on the right, which leads down to the old railway line, from where a footpath comes out on the coastal road between Thorpeness and Aldeburgh. It is now only a short walk along the beach into Thorpeness.

The Sailor's Path from Snape to Aldeburgh.

# CHAPTER FOUR

# Aldeburgh to Kessingland and Lowestoft

UNTIL the mid-sixteenth century, the port of Aldeburgh (or Old Fort) was north of the present town, where ships entered the shallow haven of Thorpe Hythe at the mouth of the Hundred river and anchored in the lee of the hill on which the church stands. Ships then became larger and the haven silted up so they approached Aldeburgh from the south up the River Alde and tied up at Slaughden. This was protected from the sea by the Orfordness peninsula, on which stands the last in the line of Martello towers. This tower has a unique quatrefoil design and had a quartet of twenty-four-pound cannons mounted on the roof supported by five similar cannons below. The fort was acquired by the Landmark Trust in 1971, a charity which rescues historic buildings in distress and gives them a future by letting them out as holiday homes.

From here I set out on the last leg of the Suffolk Heritage Coast walk to Kessingland near Lowestoft. There is not much at Slaughden (from Slog-dene meaning muddy river) but in previous centuries it must have been an intriguing and fascinating place, so precariously protected from the sea. In the sixteenth century it was a thriving port and ship building centre which by 1674 had superseded Dunwich, its rival to the north. Herrings and sprats had been the most important catches on the east coast for generations, and rents, tithes and dues were often paid with the catch. The Aldeburgh vicar received his tithe, Christ's dole, on "the wetting of the nets", whether or not any fish was caught. During the eighteenth and nineteenth centuries the cod smacks with their black hulls and white sails were a familiar sight off Slaughden. These tiny vessels sailed as far as Iceland in search of cod and to Norwegian waters for lobster and crayfish. The fish were kept alive in a well of sea water in the centre of the boat until they reached port, when they were banged on the head. The smacksmen became known as cod bangers. Later these small vessels were replaced by steam trawlers out of Yarmouth.

The shipment of coals from Newcastle along the east coast was a very early trade, and brigs, relatively large two-masted ships, called in at Slaughden. They were later replaced by faster sailing schooners, which tied up off Iken, where there were coalyards. In the last century there was a hoy passenger service from Slaughden quay to London and a steam paddle boat plied to Ipswich, whilst spritsail barges brought in coal and took away grain, malt and bricks from the Aldeburgh brickyard next to Slaughden. All have gone now, as have the warehouses, the fish-curing salt stores, the soap factory, twenty cottages and the

An idle fishing boat on Aldeburgh beach.

public house, the Three Mariners, washed away by the sea. The Three Mariners stood with its front door facing the quay, standing almost at sea level. They say they left the doors open at night to let the tide in and out! The pub finally succumbed to a violent storm in 1905. There are now two clubs at Slaughden; one is a yacht club, the other a sailing club. When asked the difference, I was informed that one was for the well-to-do and the other for the likes of you and me. My bicycle clips must have given me away!

George Crabbe, Aldeburgh's famous poet, was born in 1754, educated at Bungay and Stowmarket and at fourteen was apprenticed to a Woodbridge surgeon but had to terminate his studies to assist his drunken father run his warehouses. George then left and set himself up as a surgeon, but was not successful so took up the Cloth and became Aldeburgh's curate. He was no more successful at saving souls than he was at saving their bodies, but ended up as the parson in Trowbridge and died in 1832.

Crabbe's poems were first published in a local magazine, but it was not until Edmund Burke, an expert in political literature, took the manuscript of "The Library" to a publisher that Crabbe's poetic future was assured. He is best known for his poem "The Borough", about Aldeburgh and its fishermen, which became the basis of Benjamin Britten's opera *Peter Grimes*.

Benjamin Britten, Peter Pears and Eric Crozier were travelling across Europe with the English National Opera Group when the idea came to start up a festival at Aldeburgh where there could be performances of English music accompanied by English words. Taking opera abroad was expensive and the idea of a local festival appealed. Aldeburgh town was enthusiastic and the Arts Council promised financial help. The first Aldeburgh Festival of Music and Arts was held in June, 1948. There were recitals, Elizabethan music, a performance of Benjamin Britten's cantata *St Nicholas*, choirs, music and drama for children and exhibitions of East Anglian painters including Constable and Gainsborough.

In the early years Festival concerts were held in the Jubilee Hall, country houses, working men's clubs and churches such as Blythburgh, Framlingham, Orford and Ely. By 1960 there were sufficient funds to improve the Jubilee Hall and to purchase the Festival Club and Art Gallery in the High Street, which was opened by Prince Philip in June, 1962. Five years later the Festival moved to Snape Maltings and in 1975 the Britten-Pears School of Advanced Musical Studies was founded.

At the outbreak of the Second World War, Aldeburgh became a restricted military zone and residents were issued with special identity cards. On 10th September, 1939, the lifeboat, the *Abdy Beauclerk*, rescued seventy-four men from the *Magdapur* off Aldeburgh, the first ship to be sunk in the war. The next spring the lifeboat, with its sister boat the *Lucy Lavers*, was taking soldiers off the Dunkirk beaches. Aldeburgh sustained twenty-three air attacks, and over 160 bombs were dropped on the town.

Dr Patrick Merrick Acheson, or Dr Robin to his friends, and his wife Dr Nora became Aldeburgh's family practitioners in 1931 and Dr Robin regularly sailed on lifeboat rescue missions. When war broke out he joined up and Dr Nora remained as the sole Aldeburgh doctor. Her first wartime task was to take care of the *Magdapur* survivors. She made history by being the first woman doctor to go out on duty with the lifeboat crew, but eventually the Royal National Lifeboat Institution barred her, for her own safety, from going to sea. On one occasion a beach mine blew up, killing several children. She used a ladder to crawl across the minefield to administer morphine to the injured. When the old Cottage Hospital in the High Street was bombed, she commandeered an empty house at the back of the town and by nightfall the hospital service was operating again and she was caring for victims of an air raid. This building is still part of the Cottage Hospital. When told she deserved a medal she remarked that a battledress would be more useful.

In peace time the doctors were a familiar sight walking their pet terrier, Snooks, in the town. The dog, instead of retrieving pebbles thrown by children, unfortunately used to swallow them and eventually had to have an operation. Dr Robin died in 1959, leaving his wife to continue the practice. His patients made a collection and paid for the improvement and terracing of the children's yachting pool next to the Moot Hall, and placed a life-sized bronze sculpture of Snooks overlooking the pond.

**Left:** The bronze statue of Snooks, placed by the children's paddling pool in gratitude for the work of Dr Robin and Dr Nora Acheson.

**Right:** The Aldeburgh lifeboat, the *James Cable*.

Dr Nora continued to care for Aldeburgh people and also wrote a children's novel *Up the Steps*, based on true stories of smugglers at Aldeburgh and Thorpe. On 27th May, 1980, Dr Nora was made an Honoured Citizen of Aldeburgh in recognition of her outstanding service to the local community. She was still working at the age of eighty. A patient remarked to her, "If you go on working like this you'll drop down dead." "And that's exactly what I would wish," she replied, and on 26th February, 1981, she did just that.

The first lifeboat in Aldeburgh was named the *Pasco*. It was thirty-two foot long and pulled by twelve oarsmen. The present lifeboat, the *James Cable*, came into service in 1982. James Cable was born in 1851 and lost both his father and grandfather at sea. At thirteen he started working, for 2s 6d a week, as the cabin boy in a fishing smack. He was offered the job at eleven in morning, could not find his mother, who was at a wedding, and at one o'clock was off sailing to the fishing grounds, much against her wishes. When old enough he joined the lifeboat service and was promoted as coxswain on the *George Hounsfield* in 1888. In December, 1899, a large sea capsized the lifeboat just after launching. Twelve men swam to safety but one subsequently died. Six men were trapped beneath the upturned boat, which could not be righted even when it was beached. James Cable was not aboard as he was suffering from influenza, but his heroic efforts to cut through the beached boat failed, and the six men died. Their memorial in the Aldeburgh churchyard is marked with seven crosses. James Cable retired from the lifeboat crew in August, 1917, after fifty years' service, thirty of them as coxswain. During this time he was awarded three RNLI Silver Medals, the

Norwegian Silver Medal, the Royal Humane Society Medal and a silver box from the Mayor of Aldeburgh in recognition of his bravery in rescuing four men using his own boat. His greatest posthumous honour must be that of having the present lifeboat named after him. It now stands poised on Aldeburgh beach, at all times ready to maintain the high tradition of the lifeboat service.

The Aldeburgh Moot Hall goes back to Saxon times and was a meeting place in the centre of the town. A Moot usually administered a Hundred, which meant a hundred families or the land occupied by that number of people. The Anglo-Saxon Moots represented the first germs of popular government in England. The ground floor of this Moot Hall was open and used as a market place, as was the surrounding area complete with its Market Cross. It was here, in 1699, that poor Margaret Chantry was whipped for a whole hour having been convicted of petty theft—enough to put anyone off shoplifting. In the eighteenth century the encroaching sea swept away the Market Place, the Cross and several houses and came perilously close to the the Moot Hall.

It needs a good imagination as one walks the straight road to Thorpeness along the coast to visualize the scene in medieval times. Ships sailed through a harbour entrance somewhere along this stretch guarded by a fort with guns pointing out to sea. Now the Hundred river reaches the sea ignominiously through a culvert half way along the road near Sluice Cottage, and it is here that the Sailor's Path from Snape meets the coastal walk from Aldeburgh. A rickety old footbridge once crossed this river, known as Rattlebone Bridge, preventing pedestrians getting wet feet as they made their way to the little fishing hamlet of Thorpe. Thorpe was recorded at Domesday; it has now been absorbed into the holiday village of Thorpeness.

The river spread out into a large tidal delta and in 1908 Glencairn Stuart Ogilvie, a successful landowner, visualized this as a ninety-acre boating lake where children could play. The narrow sea entrance was dammed, the river diverted and the Meare created with islands and lagoons: a world of Peter Pan. Nowhere is the Meare more than three feet deep, and children can mess about in boats safely, sail the North West Passage, walk the plank, occupy the Smuggler's Cave, the Dragon's Den, Wendy's House or Brigand's Haunt. The lake was opened in 1912 and a Mock Tudor holiday village was built around it. Another Suffolk landmark is the House in the Clouds, a camouflaged water tank rising a hundred feet into the air. It has a pitched roof, twin chimneys and is now let out as an aerial holiday home. Near the Golf Club is the restored windmill, now a Heritage Coast centre, open to visitors during the summer months.

The village pub, the Dolphin, is in the centre of the original village of Thorpe, and from here the Heritage Coast Walk starts behind the Almshouses and meanders either along the coast or across the heath to Sizewell. Sizewell Hall is now a Christian conference centre established "to provide a place where people could get away to be with Jesus and to learn of him". The present Hall

Rowing boats for hire on Thorpeness mere.

91

The windmill and House in the Clouds at Thorpeness.

stands on the site of an earlier building, Sizewell House, which was purchased in 1859 by Alexander Stuart Ogilvie. Down the road, heading towards the sea, is the Vulcan Arms. Vulcan was the Roman god of fire who smelted iron for making armoury. It is believed that the Sizewell pub may have been associated with the nearby iron foundry and engineering works of Richard Garrett at Leiston. It is an apt name for this pub, as it stands opposite Sizewell's controversial nuclear power station—the twentieth-century Vulcan.

Construction of the power station began in April, 1961, was completed in 1966, and the power station was opened by the Earl of Stradbroke in April 1967. This power station now makes enough electricity to supply all the demands of Norwich, Ipswich and Lowestoft through the National Grid. In the thirty years the CEGB has been operating a nuclear programme, all the long-term radioactive waste that has been produced would fit into a four-bedroomed detached house. A mile away, on the outskirts of Leiston, is the District Survey Laboratory in Lovers' Lane. Here the environment is monitored continually-—land, sea and sky—for any sign of increased radioactivity in the neighbour-hood. From time to time increases have been recorded but none have come from the power station. A graph on the laboratory wall shows increased radiation levels in 1976–77 when the Chinese tested their nuclear weapons, and there is another peak in 1986 to account for the Russian disaster at Chernobyl. The survey team regularly check samples of soil, grass, sea water and the seabed, and

Geese on parade at Thorpeness mere.

they purchase local fish, examine honey and milk and check the atmosphere using Takishades. These are sticky surfaces suspended on poles, onto which the wind blows dust particles. Four outlying farms at Theberton, Darsham, Saxmundham and Friston are used as control centres to see whether increased radiation levels are general or have come from the power station. All the work done by the survey team is duplicated by the Ministry of Agriculture scientists working at Lowestoft.

Sizewell, from the Anglo-Saxon Sisa's Well, had a market in the thirteenth century and in the sixteenth was probably a small thriving port from where ships sailed to Icelandic waters. In the eighteenth century the Sizewell Gap was the place smugglers brought their contraband ashore. The landlord of the Vulcan Arms reckons there was an underground passage connecting the pub to Sizewell Hall along which the contraband passed. The Hadleigh gang was the largest and most ruthless of the gangs of smugglers who used Sizewell Gap and specialized in the illegal importation of, of all things, tea! Contraband was often hidden in vaults dug into the soft sand, especially on Leiston Common, which was desolate, remote and forbidding. The vaults were covered with planks over which was placed turf or other natural camouflage and then a flock of sheep was driven over it to remove human footprints. At Coldfair Green a vault was hidden beneath a manure heap, but when the smugglers went to retrieve their loot they were overcome with fatal fumes. The contraband, three hundred tubs of gin, was seized by Customs officers and ended up at the Excise office at Saxmundham, where it was poured away. It trickled across the courtyard out into the road, and somebody dug a hole and collected the liquor in a bucket. One man died drinking the gin, which became known as the Doomed Cargo. Mrs

93

Gildersleeves was an enterprising landlady of the Leiston White Horse. She carried kegs of brandy beneath her voluminous skirts and hid her contraband under the platform of the Meeting House of the Society of Friends.

It is a delightful walk along the path beside the sea from Sizewell to Dunwich Heath. The first part, as far as the sluice, is covered with soft springy grass among which, in summer, grows a profusion of wild flowers. Although the shortest way to Dunwich continues along the shore past the public bird hides, and a colony of breeding little terns in early summer, the more interesting way is to take the footpath from the sluice inland to Eastbridge, and then to cross the heath to the Coastguard cottages. On the left of the path stand the ruins of what is believed to be the first Leiston Abbey, founded in 1182 by Ranulph de Glanvil for the Premonstratensian Order of White Canons from Laon in France, founded in 1119. They moved inland to the present site of Leiston Abbey about the middle of the fourteenth century.

Eastbridge is delightfully remote and was a secluded haven for smugglers of the last century, even though Dragoons were permanently billeted at the the pub the Eel's Foot; the clever landlord rendered them ineffective with plenty of drink. The pub is believed to be named after a medieval priest, John Neale, who trapped the Devil in his boot and tossed this into the river. The Devil escaped in the guise of a serpent (or an eel?) and the Eel's Foot is a derivation of Neale's Boot. Eastbridge has seen many skirmishes between smugglers and Preventive Officers. The locals say that the phantom Dragoons can still be heard marching through the village—I imagine after closing time.

In 1940 Minsmere levels, drained a hundred years previously to provide rough grazing pasture, were again flooded to afford protection against an invading enemy, and the area was declared a prohibited zone. Towards the end of the war four pairs of avocets took advantage of this deserted wetland to breed. Their presence was not noted until 1947, the same year that the RSPB negotiated the lease of fifteen hundred acres of land in which to make the Minsmere Nature Reserve, opened two years later. As the wetland began to dry out the habitat became unacceptable for the avocets to breed, but in another part of the reserve the marsh harrier, one of Britain's rarest birds of prey, took up residence in the reed beds. Only here have they bred successfully and they are now a major attraction at Minsmere and jealously safeguarded.

In 1962 a scrape was constructed on the site of the old Minsmere Broad, close to the sea wall. The Broad had been created at the beginning of the eighteenth century when the mouth of the Minsmere river became blocked, but it became smaller as the land was drained and gradually disappeared. Bulldozers moved in to lower the level of the habitat to form a shallow lagoon, interspersed with small islands covered with shingle, on which the waders could breed. The salinity of the water was carefully controlled to provide brackish water of only 2 per cent salt content to encourage the reproduction of crustacea for bird feed.

The avocets appreciated this hospitality and in 1963 four chicks were reared, only one of which survived. The next year three chicks survived and then ten, and now the breeding colony of avocets is fully established. So pleased were the RSPB with their success that they adopted the figure of the avocet as their emblem. The carefully managed scrape soon attracted other breeding birds, common terns, sandwich terns, little terns, ringed plover, oystercatchers, and a common gull in 1972, the first time in Suffolk, and black-headed gulls, which are not so popular with conservationists as they will eat the chicks of other birds. The Reserve was purchased by the RSPB in 1976 and now accepts thousands of visitors each year, with a limit of one hundred per day. With so many visitors and precious avian guests to guard, a system of permits and policing is inevitable. I enjoy friendly sparrows who keep me company over a flask of tea on the heath as much as I do the fleeting sight of a marsh harrier swooping into a distant reed bed. On one occasion when I was sitting in the hide nearest the car park, I became aware of a pair of eyes fixed upon me, peering out of the dark interior of the hide. It was a swallow which had built its nest within the hide—presumably to do a bit of person watching whilst it reared its family! About two hundred species of birds are recorded annually on the reserve, half of which breed here. There is a greater variety of birds here than in any other area of comparable size in Britain.

Avocet on Havergate Island.

From Eastbridge across the heath in early autumn is a walk of incomparable colour and beauty, when the heather is at its best. Erect silver birches, the silver bark glistening as it catches shafts of sunlight, stand in a sea of magenta and purple heather. Bright yellow patches of gorse attract numerous restless butterflies. I stopped to admire a common lizard and a dragonfly, a brown aeshna, sunning themselves on a gatepost. Beside a small stream other dragonflies flitted to and fro and then rested motionless on the end of a twig or blade of grass, the same colour as themselves. There was nobody about. Peace, quiet and solitude, qualities we so often seek, all there on a warm, balmy day.

A Common Blue.                                    A Small Copper found on Suffolk heath.

**Opposite page:** Above, The Coastguard Cottages on Dunwich Heath, which now contain a tea shop. Below, fishing boats at Dunwich.

It was not until I reached Dunwich cliffs that I was brought back to reality. Cars were parked close to each other all the way along the cliff edge. This part of Dunwich Heath was donated to the National Trust by Colman's, the Norwich firm of mustard makers.

In 1286 the sea swept away much of the city of Dunwich, including Greyfriars Monastery. The storm blocked the harbour entrance with shingle.

Without the harbour the town rapidly declined and its merchant ships went elsewhere, mainly to Ipswich. Large parts of the town were abandoned and the remaining inhabitants ceased their annual job of building the walls with shingle and brushwood to protect the sandy cliffs. After 1286 these crumbled into the sea with every storm, taking with them debris of uninhabited houses and demolished churches at an average rate of a metre a year. St Leonard's Church was lost in 1300, St John's in 1540, St Peter's in 1702 and All Saints' in 1919.

I remember not so long ago standing beside the last resting place of John Brinkley Easey, marked by his gravestone in what is left of All Saints' churchyard. I went to visit the Brinkley grave again in January 1991 but discovered that it had gone over the cliff in the gales of the previous month, when large parts of the Dunwich cliffs were washed into the sea. However when I searched the undergrowth on the cliff top, I found two more gravestones. That of Jacob Forster will be the last grave in All Saints' churchyard to be washed into the sea.

Since 1921 the rate of the cliff erosion has been considerably reduced by a large sandbank (the Dunwich–Sizewell bank) that has developed off the coast, protecting the cliffs from erosion right down to Sizewell.

I listened hard, turned my head on one side, but could not hear the church bells ringing as the waves swept over them, but I am sure their sound was orchestrated with that of the sea.

I descended by steps cut into the cliff (these were also washed away in the gales during December, 1990) on to the beach, where the local fishermen were selling their catches, and watched as Stuart Bacon's team of divers brought ashore a piece of masonry they had retrieved from the seabed. In 1981 they came across what they believed to be the ruins of a church attached to the Maison Dieu Hospice. Pilgrims had come from far and wide to this hospice, as it had a cross which was believed to have remarkable healing powers.

I first came across the Dunwich Rose beside the sand dunes at Thorpeness and then on the cliffs at Sizewell. Edward Fitzgerald of Omar Khayyam fame first noted the rose in 1978 and said it had been brought by monks from the north of England, but it is a native of Suffolk. It is better known as the burnet rose (*Rosa pimpinellifolia*) as its foliage resembles those of salad burnet, whose crushed leaves smelling of cucumber and are used in salads. It is distinguished by its small, solitary, creamy-white flowers and its stems covered with numerous, closely packed, slender, straight prickles mixed with many stiff bristles. It has small, round, distinctly saw-toothed elliptical leaflets and purple-black hips in autumn. It was romanticized and popularized by the poem of James Bird:

> There blooms the heath, whose bright, though humble flower,
> An emblem shows of modest beauty's power;
> There smiles the Dunwich Rose, with snow-like blossom,
> Soft, pure and white, as is the cygnet's bosom:

This decks the stern and sterile cliff, and throws
O'er the rough brow new beauty where it grows,
Gives the proud ruggedness an aspect fair,
Like hope that brightens on the brow of care!

The Dunwich Rose.

I took the footpath out of Dunwich at the end of St James Street at Bridge Farm on the right hand side of the road. Ahead was another of the lovelier Suffolk coastal walks, which passed along the edge of Dunwich Forest to Dingle Great Hill and to the old windmill on Westwood Marshes. I walked through masses of dandelions ten feet tall, but my wife told me they were actually marsh sow thistles, very rare and found only in the south and east of England.

At the beginning of the eighteenth century these marshes were drained by a system of embankments, dykes and sluices to provide grazing land for cattle and horses belonging to Westwood Lodge Farm, described by Arthur Young as being without exception the finest farm in the country. The windmill pumped

99

water into the Dunwich river and was equipped with twelve-foot scoops on an iron wheel. Unfortunately the mill was used for gunnery practice during the last war, was then renovated but accidentally burnt down by school children in 1960.

Westwood Marshes are probably the largest uninterrupted area of freshwater reed beds in Britain and are part of the Nature Conservancy Council nature reserve at Walberswick, south of the Blyth river. Reed from Westwood Marshes is used for thatching but also provides cover for some of Britain's rarest birds: bitterns and marsh harriers nest here, while regular visitors include hen harrier, merlin and short-eared owl. Rough-legged and common buzzard are also sometimes seen. From the windmill two paths lead through the reed beds. I took the path to the right and stepped over the old railway sleepers, used to make a path through the soggy ground, and came to the River Blyth flowing through Southwold harbour. On the adjoining marsh children were taking part in the British Open Crabbing Championship. Every muddy creek and pool was surrounded by eager children lowering lumps of fish on pieces of string into murky water. Little green crabs attached themselves and were hauled to the surface and kept in buckets of water. The winner was the person who caught the heaviest crab and was awarded a "gold" medal and a cash prize. The rest received a pot of crab paste! One little girl clung possessively to a smelly cod's head she had used as bait, delightedly declaring to her disconsolate mother, "The man said I could have this too, can I take it home Mummy?"

Walberswick is a most attractive, unsophisticated, coastal village and a Mecca for artists, whose work fills the local galleries. It lacks a mountain backdrop but otherwise this could almost be a Norwegian village nesting on the edge of a fjord. The Nordic atmosphere is strongest at the harbour, where wooden buildings, once warehouses and now holiday cottages, and quays and jetties draped with floats and fishing nets, blend with fishermen's huts—some with colourful, corrugated-iron roofs. Once it was a prosperous medieval port and shipbuilding yard, even though its ships, along with those from the port of Blythburgh at the head of the estuary, were forced because of the spit to sail south parallel to the coast before reaching the sea through Dunwich Haven.

In 1328 the sea did breach the spit opposite Walberswick and since then the Blyth has flowed directly into the sea at this point. An artificial cut in the shingle was made in 1590 to form the present harbour, with the flanking piers to prevent erosion added in mid-eighteenth century. About 1757 work began to make the river navigable to Halesworth where in 1761 the first keel carrying coal tied up at Halesworth. The keels, and later wherries, were loaded from sea-going ships in Southwold harbour, although some smaller sea-going vessels reached Blythburgh Bridge. The last to do so was the Woodland Lass carrying timber to Wangford around 1870. The lighters, which carried malt, corn, coal, coke, stout and chalk, took two days for the round trip.

This navigation depended entirely on Southwold harbour being kept silt

A wind pump on the River Blyth, west of Southwold harbour.

free, however it became so silted up that carriages were able to drive across to Walberswick at low tide. Often fully laden ships had to partially unload their cargo into the wherry, the *Good Intent*, kept for the purpose before they could cross the bar into the harbour. Silting was aggravated by landowners building sea walls to reclaim land previously covered at high tide. The water that had flooded the low lying land surrounding the harbour was no longer available to flush away the silt as the tide receded. Towards the end of the nineteenth century the once bustling port was rapidly becoming the tranquil fishing village it is today.

It was near Blythburgh that King Anna was defeated and killed by Penda the King of Mercia at the Battle of Bulcamp, near Blyford, in 654. His body was carried along King's Lane to the little wooden church at Blythburgh, built it is said by St Felix in 620. Small remnants of his stone coffin are now believed to be set in the floor, between font and porch, of the present majestic church—one of the finest in East Anglia.

As the fishing industry declined smuggling flourished, a nasty, far-from-romantic business, but one that kept many peasants and labourers from starving. The Queen's Head at Blyford, now a delightfully picturesque and popular pub, claims to have been Suffolk's most notorious smugglers' inn, using the nearby church to harbour excess contraband. Customs officers raided one landlord's

101

house where the booty was stored under a four-poster bed. A child was put into the bed, her face and arms plastered with mustard and turpentine to simulate poultices for scarlet fever. The Customs officers took one look and left!

There is nothing like a good ghost story to keep prying eyes indoors at night when the smugglers are about, and the tale of Old Shuck, a large black dog with only one central eye, which was visible even when the apparition was headless, was quite enough to deter even the bravest from roaming the dark lanes. I wonder if this was the same monster, the Devil in Dog's Clothing, which ran amok biting the Blythburgh congregation in 1577 when the church was struck by lightning, killing two people and destroying the tower. The lightning scoured the main church door, but local belief was that the marks were made by the dog's claws:

> Leving the church done marvelously rented and torne, bearing ye marks as it werr of his claws or talons . . .

Ann Blackmore, an attractive wench, was found dead near Blythburgh four crossways. A black man, a drummer in the local company of Dragoons, Tobias Gill or Black Toby, lay in a drunken stupor beside her. He was duly arrested and found guilty of the girl's murder, even though he protested his innocence, and on 14th September, 1750, he was hanged.

Since then his ghost has haunted the crossroads, driving a hearse with four headless horses recklessly through the night. Was Ann murdered, throttled with a handkerchief, or did she die of fright mistaking, in the pitch night, the black drunken sailor for a dark spirit? We shall never know. Around 1970 a lorry was

Blythburgh church.

travelling at night along the undulating road across Blythburgh Common. It came to a crest in the road and the driver suddenly saw a couple, previously hidden by the hill, leading a black horse. He braked hard, stopped and climbed down from his cab, convinced that he had killed the couple, but nobody was there! This phantom couple with the horse has been seen several times on the Common in the last two hundred years. There is a story that a farmer died whilst ploughing his land and that his niece found his body lying beside his horse.

The Southwold Railway was opened in September 1879 to carry holiday, makers, although it also carried some freight and once a lion for the local circus! It connected with the main line from London to Yarmouth at Halesworth. Its "Thomas the Tank Engine" pulled six coaches along the scenic route at a maximum speed of sixteen miles per hour on a unique narrow gauge track. The train travelled so slowly, it was said, that passengers could alight from the front of the train, pick a bunch of heather and then board again at the rear! Some of the engine drivers stopped the train, set hare snares and inspected them on the return journey. The carriages, resembling those of a tramcar, had continuous wooden bench seats placed along each side of the coach. Blue cushions distinguished the First from the Third Class compartment and a ha'penny a mile extra was charged for the privilege of sitting on them. The normal Third Class fare was calculated at a rate of a penny ha'penny a mile. The carriages were not heated and on cold days the floors were strewn with ankle-depth straw. Sadly the line was closed in 1929.

Walberswick Church, built in the late fifteenth century, was once as magnificent as those at Blythburgh and Southwold, until lack of funds caused by the decline of the ship building and fishing industries at Walberswick required that a smaller church be built from the material of the larger one, which became a ruin. George Orwell, the novelist, is reported as having seen a ghost walking in these ruins.

Walking towards the village, on the left hand side of the road is the Old Manor House, the seat of the Lords of the Manor, but now more easily recognized as Mary's the well known teashop and restaurant, where it is still possible to be served with High Tea in the later afternoon. They specialize in locally caught fresh fish dishes.

The road continues through the village, where the first Suffolk Women's Institute was formed on 9th September, 1918, past several open spaces and greenswards once occupied by wooden houses destroyed in one of the great fires of Walberswick, and the small Congregational Chapel. From 1885 until 1942 a pontoon chain ferry operated by the River Blyth Ferry Co. Ltd took road traffic across the river. Originally hand powered, a donkey engine was eventually installed. Unfortunately there were times when this ferry imagined it was a submarine and sank whilst in mid-stream. Still surviving is the oldest rowing ferry in the eastern counties. For ten pence I was transported across the river, feeling like Henry VIII being rowed up the Thames! I marvelled at the strength and skill of Bob Cross the ferryman as he first rowed his boat upstream against the tide and then let it drift down to reach the other side. Halfway across I remembered with consternation that in 1616 the rowing boat capsized and the twenty-two occupants, who were returning from St James fair at Dunwich, were drowned. Happily I reached the other side safely to walk up the hill into Southwold, an attractive, soporific holiday resort where many retired gentlefolk have made their homes in the elegant houses of varied architecture, Georgian, Regency and Victorian, none of it too old as fire destroyed most of the town in 1659. Southwold developed from a small sixth-century hamlet, part of Reydon, to become in Norman times a fishing village whose only access to the sea was through Dunwich Haven to the south, but it flourished when the Blyth was made navigable, and sent more ships to Icelandic fishing ports than any other east coast port.

Bob Cross, the Walberswick ferryman.

On Gunhill cliff are the six Southwold cannons, eighteen-pounder culverins used on ships and for coastal defence. Traditionally these guns were believed to have been given to the town by the Duke of Cumberland when he returned from the Battle of Culloden having captured them from the Scots. It was related that the Duke's visit was in 1745 but the Battle of Culloden was not until 16th April, 1746! Major-General P. J. Mackesy, who has researched the problem in *The Southwold Guns* states that the guns were sent to Southwold, probably from Woolwich, in 1705. They were cast on the order of the Master General of Ordnance to be part of the town's defences against pirates and privateers. The Southwold historian, Gardner, noted for his accuracy in *The History of Dunwich*, recorded that the Duke visited Southwold on 17th October, 1745. General Mackesy agreed with this statement, but says that the Duke was probably returning to the Thames from the Continent and merely blown off course.

In 1842 when the guns were fired to honour the Prince of Wales, later Edward VII, on his birthday, the Number One gun exploded, killing James Martin, whose ghost now haunts one of the guns. At the beginning of the Second World War the townspeople prevented the guns from being melted down and turned into modern weapons. Thomas Gardner lived in Park Lane, rightly described as the most charming street in Southwold, as did diarist James Maggs and historian Agnes Strickland. The attractive but eccentric Mock Tudor/Swiss-styled house—The Studio—was once the Southwold School of Industrial Art, founded to teach fifty young men when they were not at sea.

In the Market Place stands the seventeenth-century Swan Inn, the town's principal hotel, close to the site formerly occupied by the town jail from 1711 until 1835, and opposite the Amber Shop, whose fascinating window is stocked with jewellery, some fashioned from locally found material. Amber is the fossilized resin from pine trees which grew sixty or seventy million years ago, and was then subjected to the action of sea water. Some contains flies and other insects caught in the resin whilst on the tree and then encapsulated within the amber. Locally it is believed that the darker reddish amber could have come from the resin of fruit trees. In Greek mythology amber was described as congealed tears and the Greek name, electrum, refers to its property for retaining an electrical charge when rubbed against cloth.

About eleven thousand years ago in the Stone Age, amber was used for human adornment, and has also been used to cure asthma, rheumatism and, by Roman women, to ward off witches. Although fossilized resins are found throughout the world true amber, succinite, is found only on the beaches of northern Russia and along the German Baltic coast, from where wind and tide has carried it across the North Sea and deposited it on the Suffolk shore. For generations it has been trawled into fishermen's nets or washed ashore, especially after a storm, and some local experts feel it must be indigenous. Amber, being less dense than sea water, floats ashore, getting entangled with seaweed on the high-water mark. It looks very much like a pebble before it is polished but is much lighter and will burn. Suffolk fishermen have been known to use it as a firelighter but more often have sold it to the famous amber shop in

Aldeburgh, whose history goes back to the seventeenth century. One of Queen Victoria's daughters called in at this shop to buy amber for her collection. The shop stood at the north end of the High Street near the cinema, was destroyed in the war but reopened in 1946 on the the other side of the road. It was here that Monica Mary Phillips came to work as a shop assistant. She became intrigued by amber and she has become an acknowledged world expert on the subject. In 1970 she opened her shop in Southwold and over the years has gradually acquired most of the locally available amber. Amongst her collection are two Roman amber necklaces. Her shop is now under new management.

Colonial and commercial rivalry between Holland and England, the two greatest maritime powers of the time, led to a number of sea battles off the East Anglian coast, including the Battles of Lowestoft in 1665 and Landguard Fort in 1667, when the Dutch were repulsed, and the Battle of Sole Bay in 1672, when the Dutch were victors. During May of that year a fleet of 101 English and French ships anchored in three divisions off Sole Bay. The northern division was commanded by Edward Montague, Earl of Sandwich, the central by the Duke of York, later King James II, and the French were to the south off Minsmere Haven. The two English commanders instead of remaining with their ships billeted themselves at Sutherland House (now a restaurant), which they made their naval headquarters. This fine Tudor timber-framed house, which belonged to the Elizabethan merchant, Thomas Camel, has very fine ornate moulded ceilings and was one of the few houses that escaped the great Southwold fire of 1659.

The Earl of Sandwich supposedly occupied the luxurious first floor bedroom, where he enticed a young red-headed serving wench into his bed on the eve of the battle. The Dutch surprised the English fleet, who hurriedly cut their anchor cables, leaving many of the sailors ashore in Southwold. The Earl of Sandwich, not surprisingly, overslept and the battle was already in progress by the time he boarded his flagship the St James. This caught fire during the encounter, drifted on to Easton Ness and blew up. The Earl of Sandwich was killed when he jumped from the quarter deck into the sea. The little servant girl waited in vain for his return and her ghost is still supposed to walk the corridors of Sutherland House.

Montague House in the High Street was the home of Richard and Ida Blair, parents of George Orwell, born Eric Arthur Blair, author of *Animal Farm* and *1984*. He was born in India, won a scholarship to Eton and began a career with the Burma police before returning to England to make writing his career. It is said that Eric wanted to take the name of the River Blyth as his pseudonym, but finally adopted the name of another Suffolk river to become George Orwell.

The Southwold Museum is an interesting, intimate place which displays local artefacts, some of them connected with the Southwold Railway and the Battle of Sole Bay. Across the green is the church of St Edmund, said to be the

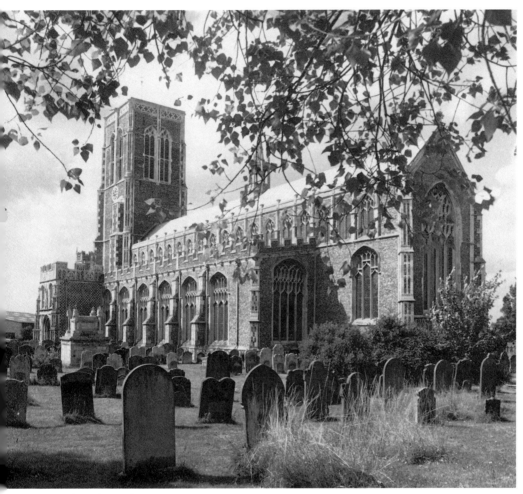

Southwold church.

finest medieval seaside church in England. It was built between 1430 and 1460 to replace an earlier wooden church which was destroyed by fire. I sometimes wonder if God is as impressed with these vast churches as we are. They are far larger than the populace of the town has ever required. Daniel Defoe, a dissenter, when visiting the town during his tour of East Anglia in 1722, remarked:

> There is but one church in this town, but it is a very large one and well built, as most of the churches in this county are, and of impenetrable flint; indeed there is no occasion

for its being so large, for staying there on Sabbath Day, I was surprised to see an extraordinary large church, capable of receiving five or six thousand people, and but twenty-seven in it besides the parson and the clerk: but at the same time the meeting house of the dissenters was full to the very doors having, as I guessed, from six to eight hundred people in it.

The church is also noted for its "Jack-smite-the-clock", known as Southwold Jack, a genuine medieval figure of a fifteenth-century man-at-arms dressed in the period of the Wars of the Roses. Operated by a cord pull, he strikes a bell with a short axe. The bell heralds the commencement of a service, or the entry of a bride at a wedding. A likeness of this Jack appears in the trademark of Adnams, the Southwold brewers, whose premises stand at the end of Victoria Street on Brewers Green.

Southwold Jack strikes an hour bell in Southwold church. Note that his armour is that of the Wars of the Roses.

For centuries ale was the staple drink of England. Tea and coffee were unknown and water frequently polluted. Each tavern brewed its own ale and

Adnams can be traced back to the Sole Bay Brewery, which was acquired by George and Ernest Adnams in 1872, originally the old brew house belonging to the Swan Inn. Their Percheron horses are truly a majestic sight, the finest in Southwold, as they pull the drays around the town delivering beer. They were reintroduced by the brewery in 1970 to offset the increasing cost of mechanized transport. Another prominent feature in Southwold is the lighthouse, of modern construction, supporting an unmanned automatic light visible seventeen miles out to sea.

The lighthouse overlooks the town of Southwold and the coastal path passes it to reach the shore.

The walk to Kessingland is along five miles of the most beautiful, unspoilt sandy beach to be found anywhere in England, formed by the sea continually washing away the soft sandy cliffs. The beach begins just north of the concrete sea wall built following the disastrous 1953 floods to prevent the sea entering Buss Creek. The shore here is all that remains of the parish of Easton Bavents which once swept out into the sea to form Easton Ness. The Easton river was navigable as far as Frostenden, three miles inland, mentioned in Domesday as being a port and having a salt pan. The Suffolk historian, Ernest Cooper, discovered the remains of a dock and quay belonging to the Viking period and there is also a burial barrow.

Early in 1986 a medieval side rudder was washed ashore at Easton Broad, six years after a similar one had been dredged up by fishermen near the same spot. Less than twenty of these rudders have been discovered in northern Europe, and those at Southwold, the only two in Britain, are dated as being made between the tenth and twelfth centuries. North European medieval ships were steered by a single rudder mounted on their starboard or steerboard, probably developed from a steering oar used to propel and steer the ship. The find of these two rudders so near to each other suggests they may have come from ships that collided and sank, perhaps in Frostenden harbour or near to it. If this is the case then there may be two ships, which sailed at the time of Domesday, waiting to be discovered.

As with most Suffolk rivers flowing into the North Sea, the longshore drift started building a spit from the northern shore blocking the mouth of the River Easton, and all that remains of that Viking estuary are Easton and Covehithe Broads. Just north of Covehithe Broad a short footpath leads inland to the fantastic ruins of another massive fifteenth-century church, completely out of proportion with the three hundred souls it once served. In 1672 the upkeep of Covehithe Church was well beyond the resources of parishioners and permission was given for Messrs Gilbert and Girling to erect a small church for one hundred and sixty people using material from the larger church, which soon became a ruin. The five bells in the tower are noted for their tone and are amongst the oldest in the country. The Redundant Churches Fund now maintains the old ruins, which have appeared several times on television.

In the fourteenth century Covehithe belonged to John de Cove, who had a quay where goods for his estate were unloaded. Covehithe's most famous citizen was John Bale, Bilious Bale to his contemporaries, who was born here on 21st November, 1495, the son of Henry Bale of Covie. John started his career as a Friar at the Carmelite Monastery in Norwich when he was twelve but soon became disenchanted with the Roman religion and became an active Protestant.

John Bale was imprisoned for his religious views at York, became friendly with Martin Luther, and wrote miracle plays and books against popery, under the patronage of Thomas Cromwell. When Cromwell died, Bale fled to Germany

The massive ruins of Covehithe church.

until the accession of Edward VI, who appointed him Bishop of Ossory in Ireland in 1552, and Bale continued to push the Protestant view to a Catholic community. The following year, when Mary Tudor came to the throne, Bale fled for his life and went to Holland, where he remained until Elizabeth I came to the throne and gave him a Prebend, or pension. John is best known for his catalogue of the illustrious writers of Great Britain, *Illustrium Majoris Britanniae Scriptorum*. He died in 1563.

Between 1878 and 1887 the sea encroached over 170 feet at Covehithe and is still rapidly swallowing up the cliffs, taking with it the road, which ends precariously balanced on the cliff top. I had to return to the beach the way I had come, and then walked beneath the cliffs along the golden dunes to the beautiful Benacre Broad, ancestral home of the Gooch family, where, in 1786, a workman found a stone bottle containing upwards of nine hundred Roman coins.

John Davie, Sea Row Jack, Kessingland's Robinson Crusoe, lived in a three-storeyed wooden tower on the shore between Benacre and Kessingland, from where he kept a lookout for ships in distress. Although well off John chose the life of a hermit, dressing in animal skins except when he entertained guests; he then changed into a swallow-tail coat, frilled shirt, breeches, hose with buckled shoes and a stove-pipe hat. He was fascinated by marine life and built up an extensive fossil collection, part of which was acquired by Cambridge University. He died in 1858, his tower was burnt down and the remainder of his fossil collection was stolen.

The port of Kessingland, its name derived from Cassing's Land or from the Scandinavian for Land of Flints, was at the time of the Conquest the most important haven between Yarmouth and Dunwich, and ancient tax returns showed that Kessingland was one of the richest places on the Suffolk coast. The Heritage Coastal Walk ends at Kessingland but there is a path which continues along the Kessingland and Pakefield cliffs in front of the caravan parks and into the busy fishing port of Lowestoft.

I chose not to take this path, but walked instead from the beach into the town to look at the church, whose pulpit is fronted by a ship's wheel, a reminder of the close affinity of this town with the sea. The Kessingland lifeboat, when it was on station until 1936, saved over 140 lives, and in times gone by Kessingland gained great wealth from the sea. Lowestoft is a noisy, traffic-congested modern town, which startled me back to reality after walking through the peaceful coastal countryside. The Heritage Coast Walk had brought me from the borders of Essex to those of Norfolk, a path weaving its way through the pages of history, from the ancient burial site at Sutton Hoo to the nuclear power station at Sizewell. All along the way pleasure can be gained from wildlife, though this is threatened severely at such places as Fagbury Point. Much of the walk is remote, secluded and an unspoilt idyllic escape from twentieth-century pressures. It must be preserved.

The *Wyvenhoe*, a spritsail barge.

# Index